SPECIAL EDUCATIONAL NEEDS

The nature of provision for special educational needs has changed dramatically over the years following the Warnock Report and the 1981 Education Act, with an increased awareness of educational needs and a focus on improving the quality of provision for much larger numbers of children. This book underpins current practice by providing necessary and relevant information about the impair- ments and disabilities which may contribute to the development of handicap and may limit educational progress.

Against a context of a generic understanding of special educa- tion, the book stresses the entitlement for all children to a broad and balanced curriculum, and explores ways in which the National Curriculum can be adapted to meet the needs of children with various handicapping conditions. The central chapters focus on particular areas of special educational needs, each chapter being written by a specialist who explores in detail how conditions can be recognised, what specialist skills and resources are needed, and the implications for provision, teacher support, curricular access, assessment and classroom management.

Ronald Gulliford is Emeritus Professor of Special Education at the University of Birmingham, and has been involved in teacher education for special educational needs since the early 1950s. His first book (with A. E. Tansley) in 1960 aimed to broaden ideas and practice in educating slow learners. *Special Educational Needs* (1971) outlined the difficulties and needs of children with various kinds of disability – it is a sign of how the field has developed that this new edition of the book requires specialist contributions. **Graham Upton** is Professor and Head of the School of Education at the University of Birmingham. He has taught in ordinary and special schools, and been involved in teacher education in colleges of education, a polytechnic and two university education departments. In addition to research conducted in conjunction with his own higher degrees, he has conducted large-scale funded research in a number of areas of special education.

SPECIAL EDUCATIONAL NEEDS

Edited by
Ronald Gulliford and
Graham Upton

London and New York

First published 1992
by Routledge
11 New Fetter Lane, London EC4P 4EE

Simultaneously published in the USA and Canada
by Routledge
a division of Routledge, Chapman and Hall, Inc.
29 West 35th Street, New York, NY 10001

Typeset in Garamond by LaserScript Limited, Mitcham, Surrey
Printed and bound in Great Britain by Biddles Ltd,
Guildford and King's Lynn

British Library Cataloguing in Publication Data

A catalogue reference for this title is available from the British Library.

ISBN 0–415–07124–0
ISBN 0–415–07125–9 (pbk.)

Library of Congress Cataloging in Publication Data

Special educational needs/edited by Ronald Gulliford and Graham Upton
p. cm.
Includes bibliographical references and index.
ISBN 0–415–07124–0. – ISBN 0–415–07125–9 (pbk.)
1. Special education – Great Britain. 2. Handicapped children –
Education – Great Britain. I. Gulliford, R. II. Upton, Graham, 1944–
LC3986.G7S67 1992
371.9′0941–dc20 92-9348
CIP

CONTENTS

CONTRIBUTORS

Keith Bovair is a Lecturer in the School of Education at the University of Birmingham.

Brian Fraser is a Lecturer in the School of Education at the University of Birmingham.

Ian Glen is Headteacher of Victoria School for the Physically Handicapped in Birmingham and an Honorary Lecturer in the School of Education at the University of Birmingham.

Ronald Gulliford is Emeritus Professor of Special Education at the University of Birmingham.

Neil Hall is a Senior Educational Psychologist in Birmingham Local Education Authority and an Honorary Lecturer in the School of Education at the University of Birmingham.

Heather Mason is a Lecturer in the School of Education at the University of Birmingham.

Carol Miller is a Lecturer in the School of Education at the University of Birmingham.

Heather Murdoch is a Lecturer in the School of Education at the University of Birmingham.

Colin J. Smith is a Senior Lecturer in the School of Education at the University of Birmingham.

Christina Tilstone is a Lecturer in the School of Education at the University of Birmingham.

Graham Upton is Professor and Head of the School of Education at the University of Birmingham.

INTRODUCTION

Ronald Gulliford and Graham Upton

The term special educational needs began to come into use in the
late 1960s as a result of increasing dissatisfaction with the terminology used in the Handicapped Pupils and School Health Service
Regulations (1945), which classified handicapped children into ten
categories according to their main handicap. There was, moreover,
an increasing awareness of the frequency of learning and other
difficulties affecting children's progress and adjustment in ordinary
schools. A book by the headteacher of an infant school (Webb,
1967) had the title *Children with Special Needs in the Infant School*
and described how 16 per cent of the 500 children who passed
through the school during a six-year period needed and were given
some additional help or consideration on account of learning, behaviour or emotional problems. The report of the Isle of Wight
survey of the education, health and behaviour of 9–11-year olds
(Rutter *et al.*, 1970) found that one child in six had a chronic or
recurrent handicap. The researchers commented that the cate-
gorizing of children according to their presumed major handicap
had now become restrictive in planning special education and suggested 'that special schooling be reconsidered from the point of
view of the actual needs of handicapped children' (p. 375). The
Report of a Working Party at the National Bureau for Cooperation in
Child Care (1970), *Living with Handicap*, suggested that categories
should be viewed not so much as a categorisation of handicaps nor
a categorisation of children but as a categorisation of special needs;
moreover, the concept of special needs should include personal and
social needs as well as more strictly educational ones (p. 206).

THE WARNOCK REPORT

In 1974 the Warnock Committee of Enquiry into the Education of Handicapped Children and Young People was set up to review special educational provision. Its report (DES, 1978) pointed out that whether a disability constitutes an educational handicap for a child depends upon many factors such as the school's expertise and resources, the child's temperament and personality, the quality of support and encouragement within the family and environment. The Report rejected the idea,

> deeply engrained in educational thinking that there are two types of children, the handicapped and the non-handicapped. Traditionally the former have generally been thought to require special education, and the latter ordinary education. But the complexities of individual needs are far greater than this dichotomy implies. Moreover, to describe someone as handicapped conveys nothing of the type of educational help and hence of provision that is required.
>
> (DES, 1978, p. 37)

The committee wished to see a more positive approach and recommended the term special educational needs, seen not simply in terms of a child's particular disability but in relation to 'everything about him (*sic*), his abilities as well as disabilities – indeed all the factors which have a bearing on his progress'.

Having considered various sources of evidence, including studies of the incidence of personal and educational difficulties in children, the committee recommended that services for children and young people should be based on the assumption that about one in six at any time and one in five at some time during their school career will require some form of special educational provision (i.e. in ordinary schools as well as in special settings). In comparison with the 1.8 per cent of children who were then attending special schools or designated special classes, this was seen as a startling conclusion although it was firmly based on evidence such as that of the Isle of Wight survey and others quoted in the Warnock Report (DES, 1978, pp. 37–9). It has, however, promoted greater attention to children with special needs in ordinary schools and more productive ways of providing for them.

The Report made recommendations about several levels of

assessment of pupils' needs: initially within the school and where deemed necessary proceeding on to multi-professional assessment – for example, where there was a likelihood of need for special provisions not normally available in ordinary schools. The importance of parents' contribution to these proposed procedures was stressed and recommendations were made about a 'Named Person' to whom parents could turn for information and guidance about the child's assessment and the recommendations made. Parents' other contributions to aspects of their children's education were emphasised in a chapter on parents as partners.

Provision for special educational needs

The Warnock Report suggested that provision for special needs was likely to take the form of one or more of the following:

1 special means of access to the curriculum through special equipment, facilities or resources, modifications of the physical environment or specialist teaching techniques.
2 the provision of a special or modified curriculum.
3 particular attention to the social structure and emotional climate in which education takes place.

It was suggested that these were not exclusive and a child may often need more than one of these forms of provision. The first of them applies particularly to children with visual, hearing, speech or physical disabilities. The second refers to the needs of children with learning difficulties but a modified curriculum may now not be appropriate as schools aim to follow the National Curriculum; the issue becomes one of modifying teaching methods and resources to take account of their varied difficulties in learning and, in the case of provision in ordinary schools, is now seen to require in-class support for learning across the curriculum. The third need is one of particular concern in special settings for pupils with emotional and behaviour difficulties in which personal support and relationships are an integral part of the special educational and therapeutic approach. It could also be said to be a necessary element in any form of integrated education. For example, the success of a special unit within an ordinary school depends upon the degree of welcome and acceptance by the staff and pupils of the school – without which the integrative purpose of such units will not be facilitated. The extent to which these forms of special provision apply in the education of pupils with different disabilities or learning difficulties can be discerned in the accounts of needs, teaching methods and resources referred to in later chapters of this book.

Three areas of first priority

The Warnock Report prefaced its summary of recommendations by identifying three areas of first priority: provision for children under 5 with special educational needs; provision for young people over 16; teacher training for special needs.

1 Nursery schools and classes have always seen an important aspect of their work as promoting the development of children who for various reasons are emotionally unsettled or retarded in speech and language or other aspects of development. A study by Osborn and Millbank (1987) found that 19 per cent of nursery schools and 30 per cent of day nurseries mentioned handicap as an influencing factor in offering a place. Apart from the general benefits of pre-school experience for children's social, intellectual and language development, there are particular ones for children with disabilities: for example, with visually handicapped children promoting the development of mobility and, where there is some useful vision, learning to respond to features of a different environment (the significance of this in relation to developmental implications for visual handicap are outlined by Chapman and Stone, 1988). For the hearing-impaired child, pre-school placements provide a valuable experience of language and a stimulus to communication. Such pre-school experiences for children with sensory disabilities are given advisory support by peripatetic teachers.

2 A number of independent colleges for the further education and training of students with sensory and physical disabilities are of long standing and provide training and preparation for employment. With reduced employment opportunities as well as increased need of provision for those with multiple disabilities, the emphasis has moved in many cases to the educational and social benefits of further education. At the same time, there has been a considerable development of provision for students with special needs in local Further Education Colleges and much discussion of curricula. Recently a White Paper *Education and Training for the*

4

Twenty-First Century (DES, 1991) was issued. Its proposals and the response of SKILL (the National Bureau for Students with Disabilities) are discussed in an article by Hutchinson (1991).

3 The Report gave considerable attention to the crucial issue of teacher education and training in relation to children with special needs. Its first recommendation was that there should be a 'special educational element' in all courses of initial teacher training. The committee saw the teaching of child development as contributing to this (for example, through the awareness of different patterns and rates of development), but their main recommendation was that a special education element should be included in all training courses so that young teachers were prepared for recognising signs of special educational needs, and knew something of the part they could play and of the role of advisory support services. This proposal was subsequently put into practice as an accreditation requirement in all courses of teacher training.

The largest group of teachers needing the opportunity for in-service special education courses are those who are concerned with special needs in ordinary schools. They are concerned with methods of support teaching, school organisation and knowledge about a wide range of difficulties in learning. The training of specialist teachers of children with particular disabilities was mainly a post-war development (apart from teachers of the blind for whom training and qualification was started in 1893; and teachers of the deaf in 1920). A specialist qualification is a requirement for teachers of the visually handicapped and for teachers of the hearing impaired. The post-war period saw the first courses leading to a qualification for teachers of children with moderate learning difficulties, emotional and behaviour difficulties and the physically handicapped followed by an increasing number of courses with a broad coverage of learning and other difficulties. In 1970, courses were established for teachers of the mentally handicapped in anticipation of the transfer of responsibility from Health to Education services. Latterly, courses have been established for teachers of children with speech and language difficulties and also for teachers of children with multi-sensory handicaps.

The practice of integrated education

The Warnock Committee described integration as 'the central contemporary issue in special education' and distinguished between three degrees of integration: locational, social and functional. The first of these refers to the placement of schools or classes for pupils with special needs within ordinary schools or in close proximity which could facilitate interaction between pupils. How far proximity leads to social integration and to participation in shared activities and experiences depends on the attitudes and understanding of staff in both settings. Special classes or units can be very separate from the main school if positive steps to encourage interaction are not taken. However, many schools for children with learning and other difficulties are set in isolated situations yet have developed relationships with local schools which have led to joint social and learning activities. Carpenter *et al.* (1988) described how an all-age school for seventy children with severe learning difficulties developed a wide range of shared social and learning activities with children in local primary and secondary schools, which led to the appointment of an 'integration teacher' – a provision extended to similar schools in the LEA. Functional integration refers to the closest form of integration where children with special needs join, part-time or full-time, the regular classes of the school. For example, one of the aims of units for hearing-impaired children in ordinary school is social and functional integration of pupils giving them experience of language in normal settings – as well as the curricular benefits. This form of provision began to be made as early as the late 1940s but accelerated in the 1960s and 1970s.

Following the Warnock Report, a number of research projects studied the working of some integration schemes. The National Foundation for Educational Research undertook a major study of seventeen programmes in fourteen LEAs; these were schemes for integrating children with learning difficulties, sensory handicaps, speech disorders or physical handicaps and links between ordinary and special schools. The aim was to identify factors of significance for integration (Hegarty *et al.*, 1982). The prime factor, as they saw it in setting up a scheme, was the headteacher's commitment to integration and capacity for enlisting the cooperation of staff. Some of the aspects which varied across the schemes were the suitability of buildings (e.g. in relation to the mobility of the physically handicapped), curricular issues and opportunities for social interaction. But the researchers' 'resounding conclusion' was that integration is possible. This was the first major book which examined the practicalities of integrated education over a wide range of settings.

Subsequent studies by the NFER have looked at other aspects of integration. Jowett *et al.* (1988), for example, investigated co-operative links between special and ordinary schools. A random sample of 268 special schools revealed that 197 schools had a current link with ordinary schools; another 31 planned, or had originally had, a link. Some 54 per cent of special school pupils and 91 per cent of their teachers or ancillaries had a regular weekly contact with an ordinary school; 39 per cent of teachers in ordinary schools paid weekly or less frequent visits to the special school. The movement of pupils was not one-way: 116 special schools had pupils coming to them, in 81 cases on a weekly basis. Norwich (1990) provides a balanced discussion of views from different perspectives about the process of integration, including the views of parents (which have not always been taken into account).

THE 1981 EDUCATION ACT

The Warnock Report was followed in 1981 by a new Education Act (implemented in 1983). The Act states that a child has special educational needs if he or she has a learning difficulty which calls for special educational provision to be made. The LEA's decision to make special provision has to be expressed in a statement which sets out the nature of the pupil's needs and the provision which is proposed, about which the parents have to be consulted – and have the right to appeal against.

Research into the implementation of the Act was carried out by Wedell *et al.* (1987). This had several stages: first, preliminary discussion with personnel in health, education and social services departments; second, detailed studies of the implementation of the Act in five localities; third, a questionnaire survey of all LEAs in England as well as studies of the role of the administrator in providing SEN services; the delivery of services in sparsely populated areas; the views of parents about their experience of the statutory assessment process. The results indicated wide variations in the proportions of children given statements and in the types of need considered eligible – e.g. some LEAs considered that any 'extra' provision must be the subject of a statement while others took the view that anything extra in mainstream was not. The allocation of resources to children with special needs tended to divert attention from those who were not given a statement. With regard to the practice of integration, three-quarters of LEAs reported placing more children in mainstream schools though in fact only 25 per cent of LEAs placed more than a quarter of children with statements in mainstream. The statutory assessment procedures were mainly administered within education departments with little involvement of other services' personnel (e.g. health and social services). The 1981 Act requires LEAs to inform parents about the procedures and their rights, as well as giving them the name of a person for information about the statementing procedures and for advice. The research found that the 'named person' was rarely contacted by parents, who preferred to consult someone they knew such as the headteacher or educational psychologist.

THE NATIONAL CURRICULUM

A report by HMI (DES, 1991) on preparations for implementing the National Curriculum for pupils with statements in ordinary and special schools was based on visits in 1989–90. It referred to a widespread commitment by teachers to planning for maximum possible access to the National Curriculum for all children. None of the schools visited was proposing to disapply any part of the National Curriculum for any pupils with statements. This is a significant finding since, in the increasing provision for pupils with special needs in recent decades, pupils with special needs have not always experienced the full range of the curriculum. There have been a number of reasons for that: those placed in special schools may have missed certain curricular experiences because the staff of a small school did not include specialist teachers of certain subjects and, as HMI often pointed out, lacked some specialist rooms and resources. Furthermore, both in special and ordinary schools, the time deemed necessary for remedying low attainment in basic skills tended to limit access to a wider curriculum.

CONCLUSION

As has been argued above, in recent years there has been a major shift in thinking about the nature and treatment of special educational needs. This reconceptualisation has taken place over a number of years and has involved a gradually evolving awareness of the limitations of the categorical system of special education introduced in the 1944 Education Act. The arguments for this change were articulated in the Warnock Report and it gained formal recognition in the 1981 Education Act where special educational needs were defined in terms of the presence of a learning difficulty rather than the existence of a handicapping condition as had been the case previously. The principal benefit of this change has been awareness of *educational* needs and a focus on improving the quality of educational provision, in both ordinary and special schools, for much larger numbers of children. It is now common to talk in terms of 20 per cent of the school population having special educational needs as compared to less than 2 per cent of children who received special education under the old categorical system.

In the context of the debate that has been generated, and especially after the publication of the Warnock Report and the passing of the 1981 Act, much has been written about the generic nature of children's special educational needs and the implications which this concept has for educational provision. The benefits which have accrued from this change have been enormous and there can be no doubt that the quality of special educational provision has been enhanced. However, as with any radical change, there is the proverbial danger of 'babies being thrown out with bath water' and the present book originates from a feeling that relevant and necessary knowledge about impairments and disabilities which may contribute to the development of handicap and which may limit educational progress have tended to be ignored in the enthusiasm for generic understanding and intervention. (See Norwich (1990) for a full discussion of this issue.) The intention here is not to argue against the new conceptualisation but to suggest that a generic approach can be made more effective if it is informed by awareness of the specific problems associated with particular impairments which some children may experience and the ways in which those problems may be responded to most effectively. Thus, in each of the chapters of the present volume an attempt has been made to consider the various conditions which give rise to special educational needs and to examine their significance for pupils' personal, social and educational development and their implications for the practice of parents, teachers and others. Each chapter has been written by a specialist in the area and it is hoped that it provides an authoritative account of the special methods and resources that may be required by pupils with particular difficulties arising from sensory or physical impairments, intellectual disabilities and emotional and behavioural problems. In each chapter an attempt is made to examine general and specific needs in relation to assessment, curriculum planning, delivery and management, the organisation of educational and other forms of provision, parent involvement, support and advisory services.

The book has been written for all teachers (including those in training) and other relevant professionals as well as for administrators and school governors whose understanding of special needs will facilitate appropriate provision. The notion that such a book will be well received by such a wide target audience is based on the contributors' experience of extensive in-service training courses and also on their awareness of the enduring popularity of Ronald Gulliford's original publication, with the present title *Special Educational Needs*. The present volume is, however, more than a second edition of that book. It has clearly used it as a model but has developed a wholly new content which is relevant to the current context. It is hoped that readers will find in it a rich source of ideas to inform their thinking and enrich their practice.

REFERENCES

Carpenter, B., Fathers, J., Lewis, A. and Privett, R. (1988) 'Integration: the Coleshill experience', *British Journal of Special Education*, 3, 3, 119–21.

Chapman, E.K. and Stone, J. (1988) *The Visually Handicapped Child in Your Classroom*, London: Cassell.

Department of Education and Science (1978) *Special Educational Needs* (The Warnock Report), London: HMSO.

Department of Education and Science (1991) *Education and Training for the Twenty First Century*, London: HMSO.

Hegarty, S. and Pocklington, K. with Lucas, D. (1981) *Educating Pupils with Special Needs in the Ordinary School*, Windsor: NFER-Nelson.

Hegarty, S. and Pocklington, K. with Lucas, D. (1981) *Integration in Action*, Windsor: NFER-Nelson.

Hutchinson, D. (1991) 'Post-school proposals and issues', *British Journal of Special Education*, 18, 3, 97–9.

Jowett, S., Hegarty, S. and Moses, D. (1987) *Joining Forces: a Study of Links Between Ordinary and Special Schools*, Windsor: NFER-Nelson.

Ministry of Education (1945) *Handicapped Pupils and School Health Service Regulations*, London: HMSO.

National Bureau for Cooperation in Child Care (1970) *Living with Handicap*, London: NBCC.

Norwich, B. (1990) *Reappraising Special Needs Education*, London: Cassell.

Osborn, A.F. and Millbank, J.E. (1987) *The Effects of Early Education*, Oxford: Clarendon Press.

Rutter, M., Tizard, J. and Whitmore, K. (1970) *Education, Health and Behaviour*, London: Longman.

Webb, L. (1967) *Children with Special Needs in the Infant School*, London: Colin Smythe.

Wedell, K., Welton, J., Evans, J. and Goacher, B. (1987) 'Policy and provision under the 1981 Act', *British Journal for Special Education*, 14, 2, 50–3.

1

CURRICULUM ISSUES

Keith Bovair

In a language lesson, Kathleen sits, listening attentively to her teacher. French is the spoken word and the conversation is focused on the lunch being served. There is cheese, bread and lemonade. The object of the exercise is to greet the teacher with the word 'Bonjour', to request an item on the table and to say, 'Merci'.

There are approximately six other pupils in the class and the teacher and her assistant are busy speaking to each one. Kathleen is keen to get their attention and says very clearly, 'Excusez moi, Pardon'. The teacher does not hear this, but soon turns to her for the greeting, the request and the reply and the thank you, which Kathleen produces successfully and elicits the reply from the teacher of 'Bon'.

This exercise was videotaped and when the teacher reviewed it, she was surprised to hear the extended language Kathleen had picked up by listening to the teacher and assistant speaking. This is not uncommon in classrooms, but what was surprising was that Kathleen is a pupil who attends a school for children with severe learning difficulties and is participating with pupils from a school for children with moderate learning difficulties in a Modern Language lesson where she will obtain the same certificate of achievement as children in mainstream schools. This same young person would have been totally excluded from this experience if she had been educated in the very early 1970s; so would the children with whom she was sitting. Prior to 1971, she would probably have been excluded from any type of education, with the exception of self-help and care.

The Education Reform Act of 1988 established the principle that every pupil in maintained schools is entitled to a relevant, broad, balanced and differentiated curriculum. It identified three core areas of the curriculum – English, Maths and Science – and the foundation areas of History, Geography, Technology, Music, Art, Physical Education and a Modern Foreign Language; it can be delivered through cross-curricular schemes of work or modules. The intent of this was to bring clarity and continuity of learning to the British educational system and to raise standards by an injection of political rhetoric and a new legislated framework.

What was not expected by the new education reformers was that educators in special education would take up the challenge which it laid down. Children with special educational needs, who were once dealt with on the fringes of education, had legislated for them the right to a curriculum that was being offered to those children who were in the mainstream of education. This new legislation provided special educators an opportunity to turn the rhetoric of the architects of the 1988 Education Act into reality (Ashdown *et al.*,1991).

Her Majesty's Inspectors had actually fuelled enthusiasm about the curriculum in their Education Matters series, *Curriculum from 5 to 16* (DES, 1985a). The following definition, for example, was invigorating for special educators who were trying to extend the curriculum for all children, but particularly, those with special educational needs:

A school's curriculum consists of all those activities designed or encouraged within its organisational framework to promote the intellectual, personal, social and physical development of its pupils. It includes not only the formal programme of lessons, but also the informal programme of so-called extra-curricular activities as well as those features which produce the school's ethos, such as the quality of relationships, the concern for equality of opportunity, the values exemplified in the way that the school sets about its task and the way in which it is organised and managed.

(Whitaker, 1988, p. 20)

As Whitaker (1988) pointed out:

such a definition promotes an inclusive view of curriculum design and suggests an altogether more holistic approach than

14

we have been traditionally used to. It was a statement seen by educators in special education that helped encourage the opportunity for inclusion of pupils with special educational needs into the mainstream of curriculum opportunity by pointing to 'the equality of opportunity'.

(Whitaker, 1988, p. 21)

However, Sexton (1991) suggests a more cautionary, if not jaundiced, view of the key words used in proposals for curriculum reform:

> those euphemisms 'relevant', 'balanced' and 'broad', so readily trotted out, originated with the HMI (Her Majesty's Inspectorate). Relevant meaning parochial, limiting the child to his or her immediate experience; balanced meaning shying away from clear conclusions or statements; broad meaning a smattering of everything and a clear knowledge of nothing.

(Sexton, 1991, p. 20)

This view might well have applied to the curriculum in some special schools though there had long been debate about how to turn such concepts into reality. In the area of learning difficulties, Segal (1963) and Tansley and Gulliford (1960) had discussed the type of curriculum that would meet the needs of the population of pupils who experienced a disability of mind and body. Each identified key curriculum areas; Segal saw basic skills, citizenship, safety, health and hygiene, religious and moral education, leisure, vocational guidance and science as key areas of the curriculum. Tansley and Gulliford identified oral and written language, number, creative and practical work, religious education, knowledge and awareness, physical education and social competence as broad curriculum areas with the core of the curriculum being language and number. Unfortunately, for a long period of time, special schools and units stayed with the core of language and number, narrowing the vision that Tansley and Gulliford offered; one that recognised 'a periphery of additional knowledge about the environment, creative and aesthetic activities, and practical interests' (Wilson, 1981, p. 12). Instead specialist settings and schools tended to provide a deficiency based curriculum as described by Swann (1988) and Bovair (1989). Typically, the deficiency based curriculum was based on English, Maths, PE and Art under the guise of project work

15

(Bovair, 1989) although it might be extended by the particular interest of the staff employed at some time in a specialist setting or special school. Often, however, when these staff involved moved on, so did the interest area. This is still experienced in relation to subjects such as modern languages in special schools.

THE WARNOCK REPORT

Interest in the education of children with SEN was accelerated by the publication of the Warnock Report (DES, 1978) which was seen as compensating for the marginalisation of children with special educational needs which had gone before. In curriculum terms, the Warnock Report encouraged a set of twofold goals of education. They are:

> different from each other, but by no means incompatible. They are, first, to enlarge a child's knowledge, experience and imaginative understanding, and thus his awareness of moral values and capacity for enjoyment; and secondly, to enable him to enter the world after formal education is over as an active participant in society and a responsible contributor to it, capable of achieving as much independence as possible. The educational needs of every child are determined in relation to these goals.
>
> (DES, 1978, p. 5)

This pro-active statement, which saw the individual as a partici- pant rather than a receiver of care and education, encouraged special educators to begin to test and stretch the boundaries of their previous educational and caring worlds.

Brennan's writings (1979, 1985, 1987) tackled the systems, structures and content of the curriculum during this time. He showed how to ensure that children could have access to a wide curriculum and still have their individual needs met by individual programming as in the example he gave of John.

> John is severely physically disabled. He has no legs or arms and his mobility is totally dependent on a wheelchair. He requires assistance, not only to move around the comprehensive school, but also to move around the classroom. His school timetable must be carefully organized so that the

support he requires is capable of ensuring he is in the right place at the right time. Once there he learns normally in academic subjects though he requires special help with recording. School progress is satisfactory. John has successful GCE 'O' level studies behind him and is continuing at 'A' level.

(Brennan, 1985, p. 35)

At the same time as interest in the development of curriculum for children with special educational needs was growing so was the interest in greater integration of this population of children into ordinary school settings. Also observations and criticisms had emerged about the limitations of the curriculum in special schools and classes. It was identified as being narrow and repetitive (DES, 1978). These criticisms were justified but recognition that specialist settings were extending their relationship with their educational community were either ignored or seen as an attempt to protect the existence of the special school. The field felt the pull of this duality of 'either – or' during the 1980s. Either you segregate children or you integrate seemed to be the only possibilities. Yet as was being discovered by the practitioners in the field, a common ground was being established by special educators working with their colleagues in ordinary schools.

This recognition of overlap and extension of opportunity was accelerated by the interpretation of the 1981 Education Act and its supposed focus on integration, stating that whenever feasible a child with special educational needs should be educated within the mainstream. Educators in special education were taking their experiences of individualising the curriculum and transferring these skills to a wider curriculum area.

Those working in specialist settings were looking at ways and means to expand educational opportunities for children with special educational needs. They were also changing their roles to become active in the provision of outreach and support for their colleagues in ordinary schools, the management of which was often complex (as identified by Baker, 1989) and under-resourced. However, special schools pursued outreach in various guises (Day, 1989) and several took on the challenge of the extension of the curriculum by a closer collaboration with ordinary schools.

The collaboration was assisted by the Technical and Vocational Educational Initiative (TVEI) which encouraged skills of direct value at work, equipping students to enter the world of employment, to develop problem-solving skills and establishing a bridge from school to work through relevant activities. It also created a forum in which special schools sat alongside secondary schools and further education to work collaboratively on projects within the guide-lines of TVEI. Money was made available to establish in-service training (TVEI Related In-Service Training – TRIST) for all staff involved, and it was here that a strong common ground was well established, leading to exchanges of ideas, of resources and of students and staff between the different kinds of establishments. Other ventures into curriculum development followed in the wake of this initiative. Collaboration over GCSE course work and shared facilities were assisted by a new way of grouping schools. *Clusters* of schools were set up to work together in their education communities and when primary schools entered into this world under the guise of Grant Related In-Service Training (GRIST) (often considered by educators as TRIST without money), a healthy relationship benefited all children. This included moving from further education placements to projects where, for example, secondary age children from a special school with learning difficulties piloted a reading project related to children's books, in which they went and read to children in infant schools. Hinchcliff and Renwick (1989) describe curriculum development in their special school, pointing out that they took as their starting point the premise stated in *Better Schools* (DES, 1985b) that curriculum 'whether at an ordinary school or a special school' should be broad, balanced and differentiated and turned this into reality. They point out how they extended the curriculum from one which was deficiency-based to one which not only occurred in the special school, but took place in ordinary primary, secondary and further education settings, along with the use of community resources, such as dance studios, art museums, photographic studios, etc. They also point out that this extension not only offers opportunities for children but that the cooperation between teachers, together with the opportunities which it offers for observing other educational situations and practices, broadens thinking about the curriculum.

This model accepted Brennan's (1985) vision that students should experience as much of a common curriculum as is feasible with special schools replicating mainstream curriculum as much as possible. Bovair (1989) goes further than replication; rather than being *apart from* the curriculum that exists in ordinary settings, Bovair promotes the concept of being *a part of* that curriculum, accessing the ordinary setting to extend opportunities for children considered to have SEN.

ENTITLEMENT FOR ALL

The development of special schools in the 1980s found them designing parallel curricula which would enable children to transfer from the special to the ordinary school setting. In establishing a closer relationship with schools in their educational community, the possibilities for children to extend their curriculum opportunities while preparing for a possible return to mainstream, have been a focus of this period. Unfortunately, the move towards greater integration was seen by many as being threatened by the introduction of the National Curriculum. In September 1987, the Special Educational Needs National Advisory Council wrote:

> The major developments from which we have drawn encouragement during the past decade include the Warnock Report (DES, 1978), the Education Act 1981 (DES, 1981), and the Third Report of the Committee for Education, Science and Art (House of Commons, 1987), together with the positive responses to these of many LEAs and individual schools. Although the unevenness of responses and the inadequacy of funding for improved teacher–pupil ratios and in-service education leave much to be achieved, there was a reason to hope that progress required by law would continue. However, our reading of the consultative document leads us to fear that the interests of children with special educational needs could suffer a set-back. The consultation document makes only one reference to the individuals with LEA statements of special educational needs and provision. We ask that the existing legislation and related recommendations, together with the philosophy which underlies these, are taken fully into account in legislation for a national curriculum and for the management of schools.
>
> (Haviland, 1988, pp. 60–1)

Avoiding either a reactive or an inactive response, educators in special education took a pro-active response by lobbying the appropriate bodies, first to ensure that special education was included in the actual Reform Act and the subsequent documentation which supported it. The outcomes of this were key documents from the National Curriculum Council. A brief but concise *Circular 5* (NCC, 1989a) redressed the 'error' of neglecting the area of special educational needs and emphasised the principle of participation in attainment targets and programmes of study for all pupils. Following in the wake of this document, *A Curriculum for All* (NCC, 1989b) established that 'All pupils share the right to a broad and balanced curriculum, including the National Curriculum' (p.1) while *The Whole School Curriculum* (NCC, 1989c) identified the opportunities for children with special educational needs in light of this new curriculum. Ashdown *et al.* (1991) point out that, 'Through its discussion of cross-curricular skills, dimensions and themes, it puts to rest many of the fears of the special educator that the pupil with learning difficulties may be forced to follow an arid academic curriculum' (p.14). It took the principles of *A Curriculum for All* into the regions of curriculum for direct experience of industry and the world of work, for opportunities to develop self awareness under the umbrella of careers education and guidance, and to develop an appreciation and understanding of responsibilities to the community and to promoting positive and responsible attitudes towards the environment (NCC, 1989b).

The cross-curricular themes are seen by many as the way ahead for the special educator,

> for it is here that curriculum compatibility can be achieved. The cross-curricular skills, dimensions and themes should form the bed-rock upon which we set the core and foundation subjects of the National Curriculum. . . . We can find many of the curriculum activities which we have considered crucial to the education of pupils with learning difficulties. What is more, these activities are given status and are accepted in their own right as valid and valuable. It will be possible to state openly where the themes are contributing to the total educational package for the pupil. Indeed, the curriculum weighting towards these themes may be greater for the pupil with special educational needs.
>
> (Ashdown *et al.*, 1991, pp. 14–15)

ASSESSMENT AND TESTING

Assessment in special education has often meant ascertainment of a special educational need as part of a statutory requirement to enable decision makers to make decisions about the resources to which an individual is entitled. This entitlement has then been enshrined in a Statement of Special Educational Need. But 'while many of the children defined by the Warnock Report as having SEN would have been assessed on a multi-disciplinary basis, only some one in ten of them became the subjects of statements' (DES, 1991). Furthermore, the population of children with special educational needs is a fluctuating one and does not stand still or become frozen in time by a 'statement'. Issues of what form assessment takes needs to be considered in relation to a diverse population of pupils. The present recommendations framed within the 1988 Education Reform Act raise many concerns for those responsible for children with special educational needs and those educators in ordinary education.

In relation to testing, Eric Bolton, then Chief Inspector HMI, made a recent observation about his concern over testing and its relationship to a national curriculum. Having looked at the United States and their approach to this area he commented:

> America is in a hell of a mess, particularly over testing and exam scores. The machine marked 'testing' has left America saying, 'where did the curriculum go?'. Although test scores go up every year, what kids know goes down. We must avoid that.
>
> (cited by Tester, 1991)

Assessment as an area of educational evaluation began, as Rouse (1991) points out, as a field 'dominated by psychometrics' (p. 296). The psychometricians and their relation with schooling were seen by Schostak (1983) as those 'pleased to study the individual as a summation of individual differences – a bundle of deviations from population norms. In this way they ignore individuals completely, seeing IQ scores, personality scores, attitude scores – dividing the individual into shreds' (p. 5). Are the purposes behind the 'shredding' a means to rationalise the movement of an individual from one educational placement to another? Is it a means to appease a conscience which knows that if the appropriate resources (often those of time) were in place, individuals could have their

21

educational, physical and social needs met without their loss of dignity?

Rouse argues that assessment has moved from 'assessment of the learner's ability, aptitude and deficits which involved ranking and comparison' to

> assessment of the learner of the curriculum against pre-determined criteria . . . assessment of the curriculum and its delivery involving learners in their own assessment, . . . teachers becoming reflective practitioners assessing not only the learner but also themselves, the curriculum and the classroom context.
>
> (Rouse, 1991, p. 293)

This positive move could be in danger in the present educational climate. The concern of limiting life opportunities through the misuse of assessment has been the concern of a wide range of professionals in mainstream and special education. The case of Terry gives an example of professionally imposed limitations.

> Terry, who at the age of eight, was referred to a school under the old label of Educationally Sub-Normal – Mild, (ESN (M)). He was tested and assessed and placed 'appropriately' by IQ measurement in the special school. During the early days of observation, testing and assessment, this young man listened and bore witness to conversations that informed him that he was 'backward'. Terry's self-image was distorted although he was a capable young boy, who fortunately, through his efforts and the advocacy of educators, could at the end of his educational career return to his local community, and pass many of the exams that he was almost excluded from
>
> (Bovair, 1990, pp. 5–6)

Writers such as Ainscow (1988), Rouse (1991) and Wedell (1991) have asked the question, 'Why do we assess?'. A possible answer is that assessment is a means to identify a pupil's present level of attainment and to look to future instructional needs. The use of assessment should investigate the effectiveness of the education provided and encourage a review of the curriculum. The inter-relation of assessment and curriculum should ensure that those with individual needs have access to a broad, balanced and differentiated curriculum. Far too often though, assessment has occurred at the beginning of children's entry into special education and again towards the end of their time in special education. The Warnock Report recommended that 'The progress of a child with special educational needs should be reviewed at least annually' (para. 4.53). In reality, the nature of the need should dictate a daily, if not weekly review but all too often the regular monitoring recommended in the Warnock Report amounts to little more than establishing yearly reading and mathematical ages with a generalised annual report. It should also be noted that this narrow focus has been influenced in a manner

> that in search for special forms of education, assessment strategies have been developed that disregard what teachers already know about their pupils. What is needed, therefore is a return to some old ideas; solutions which emphasise natural means of gathering information by informal observation, questioning and discussion.
>
> (Ainscow, 1988, p. 152)

The Task Group on Assessment and Testing (TGAT) (DES, 1988), was set up by the Secretary of State to make recommendations about how children's progress in the subjects of the national curriculum should be assessed. In relation to children with special educational needs the report states that

> Like all children, those with special educational needs require attainable targets to encourage their development and promote their self-esteem. We therefore recommend that, wherever children with special educational needs are capable of undertaking national tests, they should be encouraged to do so.
>
> (DES, 1988, Sect. 169)

Testing is the main part of assessment in the new ERA, yet it needs to be recognised that 'testing may be a part of a larger process known as assessment; however, testing and assessment are not synonymous. Assessment in educational settings is a multi-faceted process that involves far more than the administration of a test' (Salvia and Ysseldyke, 1985, p. 5). TGAT goes on to state that:

> The national tests themselves should be designed so as to be appropriate to children across the whole ability range,

modified as necessary for children with particular sensory problems (ie blind and partially sighted children, deaf and partially hearing children) and those with communication difficulties.

(DES, 1988, Sect. 168)

In summary, curriculum and assessment have often been viewed as two different activities, yet those experienced in meeting the individual needs of pupils in special and mainstream educational settings see that one purpose of assessment is to enable educators to review the appropriateness of the education being offered and to develop the curriculum. This is the challenge.

CONCLUSION

Within the National Curriculum, the period of compulsory education is divided into four key stages. At the conclusion of each Key Stage, children will be formally assessed by a series of Standard Assessment Tasks (SATs) which show their level of attainment. Parents will be informed annually of the progress their child has made; a fairly straightforward process, which on the surface seems fair and sensible, yet at what cost? This information will be available for all to compare and could encourage a league table attitude between schools, and most damaging, between children. Although attempts have been made to play down this possibility, the nature of it all precludes any platitude that it will harm no one, only enhance educational opportunity. But if the National Curriculum is to be an enhancing mechanism for educational opportunity, why are there exclusion clauses for children identified as having special educational needs? (Sect. 19, 1988 Education Reform Act). A curriculum for all should be all-encompassing. It should reverberate with the hopes and aspirations of all the individuals it pertains to; not to say it is for some, but not for others.

What is required of any educators is the ability to consider individuals and the opportunities which need to be extended to them in order that they may have access to a 'broad, balanced and differentiated curriculum'. It needs to be prepared to recognise as Male and Thompson point out

(a) the effect of not receiving and absorbing all the information offered;

(b) the effect of finishing work more slowly and therefore not completing a task before starting the next one;

(c) the effect of their inability to transfer learning from one situation to another.

(Male and Thompson, 1985, p. 13)

They go on to point out that adaptations will be necessary in assessment methods, materials, organisation, and the use of personnel to accommodate the individual needs of pupils. The value of this was seen in the case of John (cited above) who had a successful educational experience when time, resources and energy were used to meet his needs.

With the National Curriculum, a common framework and a common language has been identified. In order to extend the educational experiences for all pupils, we need to establish a common ground where individual needs can be discussed, planned for and accommodated within education and where children like Kathleen (mentioned at the beginning of this chapter) can say about the national curriculum, 'C'est pour moi'.

REFERENCES

Ainscow, M. (1988) 'Beyond the eyes of the monster: an analysis of recent trends in assessment and recording', *Support for Learning*, 3, 3, 149–53.

Ashdown, R., Carpenter, B. and Bovair, K. (1991) *The Curriculum Challenge, Access to the National Curriculum for Pupils with Learning Difficulties*, Lewes: Falmer Press.

Baker, D. (1989) 'Headteacher: architect of change or victim of events?', in D. Baker and K. Bovair (eds) *Making the Special School Ordinary, Vol. One, Models for the Developing Special School*, Lewes: Falmer Press.

Bovair, K. (1989) 'The special school, a part of, not apart from the educational system', in D. Baker and K. Bovair (eds) *Making the Special School Ordinary, Vol. One, Models for the Developing Special School*, Lewes: Falmer Press.

——(1990) 'This isn't Kansas, Toto', in D. Baker and K. Bovair (eds) *Making the Special School Ordinary, Vol. Two, Practitioners Changing Special Education*, Lewes: Falmer Press.

Brennan, W.K. (1979) *The Curricular Needs of Slow Learners*, London: Evans/Methuen Educational.

——(1985) *Curriculum for Special Needs*, Milton Keynes: Open University Press.

——(1987) *Changing Special Education Now*, Milton Keynes: Open University Press.

Day, A. (1989) 'Reaching out: the background to outreach', in D. Baker and

K. Bovair (eds) *Making the Special School Ordinary, Vol. One, Models for the Developing Special School*, Lewes: Falmer Press.

Department of Education and Science (1970) *Education (Handicapped Children) Act*, London: HMSO.

——(1978) *Special Educational Needs* (The Warnock Report), London: HMSO.

——(1979) *A View of the Curriculum*, London: HMSO.

——(1981) *The Education Act of 1981*, London: HMSO.

——(1985a) *Curriculum from 5 to 16*, London: HMSO.

——(1985b) *Better Schools*, Cmnd. 9469, London: HMSO.

——(1989) *National Curriculum: From Policy to Practice*, London: HMSO.

——(1991) *Special Needs Issues*, London: HMSO.

Department of Education and Science and Welsh Office (1988) *National Curriculum Task Group on Assessment and Testing: A Report*, London: HMSO.

Gulliford, R. (1971) *Special Educational Needs*, London: Routledge and Kegan Paul.

Haviland, J. (ed.) (1988) *Take Care, Mr Baker*, London: Fourth Estate.

Hinchcliff, A. and Renwick, C. (1989) 'Curriculum development in one special school', in D. Baker and K. Bovair (eds) *Making the Special School Ordinary, Vol. One, Models for the Developing Special School*, Lewes: Falmer Press.

House of Commons (1987) *Special Educational Needs: Implementation of the Education Act 1981*, Third Report from the Education Science and the Arts Committee, Session 1986–87, London: HMSO.

Jackson, B. and Marsden, D. (1986) *Education and the Working Class*, London: Routledge and Kegan Paul.

Male, J. and Thompson, C. (1985) *The Educational Implications of Disability*, London: The Royal Association for Disability and Rehabilitation.

NCC (1989a) *Circular Number 5, Implementing the National Curriculum – Participation by Pupils with Special Educational Needs*, York: National Curriculum Council.

——(1989b) *Curriculum Guidance Two: A Curriculum for All*, York: National Curriculum Council.

——(1989c) *Curriculum Guidance Three: The Whole Curriculum*, York: National Curriculum Council.

Rouse, M. (1991) 'Assessment, the National Curriculum and special educational needs: Confusion or Consensus?', in R. Ashdown, B. Carpenter and K. Bovair (1991) *The Curriculum Challenge, Access to the National Curriculum for Pupils with Learning Difficulties*, Lewes: Falmer Press.

Salvia, J. and Ysseldyke, J. (1985) *Assessment in Remedial and Special Education*, 3rd edn, Boston: Houghton Mifflin.

Schostok, J.F. (1983) *Maladjusted Schooling*, Lewes: Falmer Press.

Segal, S.S. (1963) *Teaching Backward Pupils*, London: Evans.

Sexton, S. (1991) 'Take these inspectors to task', *Times Education Supplement*, p. 20, 17 May 1991.

Swann, W. (1985) 'Is the integration of children with special educational needs happening?: An analysis of recent statistics of pupils in special schools', *Oxford Review of Education*, 11, 1, 3–18.

——(1988) 'Learning difficulties and curriculum reform: integration or differentiation?', in G. Thomas and A. Feiler (eds) *Planning for Special Needs*, Oxford: Basil Blackwell.

Tansley, A.E. and Gulliford, R. (1960) *The Education of Slow Learning Children*, London: Routledge and Kegan Paul.

Tester, N. (1991) 'The troublesome priest', *Education*, 177, 25, 21 June 1991.

Wedell, K., (1991) 'Questions of assessment', *British Journal of Special Education*, 18, 1, 4–6.

Whitaker, P. (1988) 'Curriculum considerations', in D. Hicks (ed.) *Education for Peace*, London: Routledge.

Wilson, M.D. (1980) *The Curriculum in Special Schools. Schools Council Programme 4 Individual Pupils*, London: Schools Council.

2

MANAGEMENT OF SPECIAL NEEDS

Colin J. Smith

Any discussion of the management of present provision for meeting special educational needs must start by posing the question whether schools and teachers will be able to meet special needs within the spirit of the 1981 Education Act while meeting the demands made by the 1988 Education Act and its attendant reforms? What are the implications of recent changes for Local Education Authorities, primary, secondary and special schools? What are the questions which should be addressed at each of these levels if management is to be effective in coping with change?

THE SPIRIT OF 1981

The 1981 Act itself did not fully realise the implementation of the broader concept of special education envisaged by the Warnock Report (DES, 1978). Instead of identifying resources for providing access to the curriculum, appropriate teaching and a suitable educational environment, the 1981 Act has been criticised for concentrating on the identification of children whose educational progress compares unfavourably with that of most children of their age group (Brennan, 1987). This emphasis on determining whether these children have 'a significantly greater difficulty in learning' has focused attention on the 2 per cent of children who require the protection of a formal written statement of special educational needs, rather than the 18 per cent of other pupils who, according to the Warnock Report, would require special education at some time in their school career.

Even the potential power of a formal statement, which holds a Local Educational Authority accountable to child, parent and community for its allocation of resources towards the equitable treatment of pupils with difficulties or disabilities which hinder educational progress, according to one major research study has been 'rendered impotent by the use of vague and generalised descriptions of children's needs and the provision required to meet those needs' (Goacher *et al.*, 1988, p. 152).

There has also been a continued focus on available rather than appropriate provision. Official advice on the assessment of special educational needs (DES, 1983; DES, 1989) suggests that assessment should be based on a careful collection and analysis of multi-professional opinion, which delineates a specific programme of specialised teaching and the equipment and facilities necessary to implement it. Only after this formal recording of needs should attention be given to the best place for its delivery, with a presumption that whenever possible this should be in an integrated mainstream setting. In practice, as Fish (1989) points out '*where* children are to receive special education has taken precedence over *what* they are to receive' (p. 20).

Thus possibilities for placement appear to have determined the content of some statements, instead of the original intention that the best possible provision should be determined before examining where this might be delivered. Too often the management decision has not been about what is best for children but where is a suitable place to put them and all too easily this slips back into thinking in terms of categorical labels rather than individual needs. As research by Goacher *et al.* (1988) shows, 'contributors to statements find difficulty in separating the specification of needs from the provision required to meet needs, and they tend to pay little attention to anything other than within-child factors' (p. 152).

These criticisms show that the 1981 Act fell some way short of the broader concept of special education advocated by the Warnock Report but the Act did encourage a move towards a more relative and interactive assessment of what schools can offer pupils with special needs and how the educational environment can be adapted, rather than looking only at what are the physical, intellectual or emotional disabilities which might be seen as deficits within the child. When the Act was implemented in 1983, the attendant publicity and a considerable investment in providing in-service training for teachers in ordinary schools alerted everyone to the view that *special needs* was not a term to be applied only to the 2 per cent of children who might be *statemented*, to use that ugly, depersonalising but now inescapable addition to educational jargon. It was now widely accepted that a much larger group of about 18 per cent of children would need special educational help at some time in their school careers. Most of these children were pupils with difficulties in learning and behaviour in ordinary schools and often their problems arose from a mismatch between their present stage of development and teacher expectations engendered by an inappropriate curriculum (Booth *et al.*, 1987).

While the formal assessment of the *2 per cent* continued to place an emphasis on clinical diagnosis and additional and frequently separate provision, for the *18 per cent* there was an acceptance that meeting their needs was the responsibility of all teachers within a school: a view encapsulated by the slogan, 'every teacher is a teacher of special needs'. It also created what Gross and Gipps (1987) describe as 'an atmosphere in which LEAs protected their special needs services and cut elsewhere' (p. 213).

The question at issue now is whether more recent reforms have created a different atmosphere in which LEAs and individual schools may be less sympathetic towards finding the resources for supporting effective special education. Has the spirit which stimulated changes in attitude and thinking been curbed by the effects of more recent reforms?

Managers at different levels might address some more specific questions about how much progress has been made towards the achievement of the broader concept of special education advocated by the Warnock Report and supported by the initiatives which followed the implementation of the 1981 Act.

1 Administrators might consider whether policies for assessment do respond with sensitivity to individual needs.
2 Teachers in primary and secondary schools might look at whether their schools have changed to provide a more inclusive education accepting the common needs of children who might previously have been segregated from the mainstream.
3 Teachers in special schools might reflect on whether their schools now work more closely with others to promote the perception that as Fish (1989) puts it 'there is only one population of children, some of whom have disabilities and

special educational needs. There are not two populations, the hale and the handicapped, or the ordinary and those with special educational needs' (p. 15).

These suggested topics are offered as illustrative examples, many other questions will come readily to mind; the important point is that management decision making should be informed by a perception of progress towards long-term aims and not merely be reactive to new developments.

THE EFFECT OF RECENT REFORMS

The 1988 Act has considerable implications for how pupils with special educational needs are viewed by their schools. The idea of the entitlement of all children to participate in the National Curriculum should be a positive step towards integration and 'normalisation' for pupils with special needs. On the other hand, there may be less positive consequences following from age-related testing on attainment targets, which offer little prospect of clearly evident annual progress beyond the early levels for pupils with difficulties in learning.

Some pupils may be exempted from the National Curriculum or certain parts of it for a temporary period but continued *exception* will require a formal statement of special educational need. There is a possibility that this will renew the stigmatisation of less able children formerly associated with streaming, at the very least it is likely to mean a retreat from the acceptance that all teachers should accept responsibility for meeting special needs. This view will be further reinforced by suggestions that in future only children with special educational needs, presumably officially verified by formal statements, will be permitted to use dictionaries in GCSE examinations. Such clear signals that special consideration entails special designation do bring into question whether implementing the National Curriculum takes sufficient account of the requirement for varied and adaptable approaches to teaching for many more pupils than those protected by a formal written statement.

New administrative arrangements such as local management of schools and open enrolment with their underlying philosophy that 'money will follow the pupil', will also have consequences for the way schools view their responsibility for pupils with special educational needs. As Caldwell (1989) suggests, arriving at a formula for funding which is 'attractive to schools to meet special needs but will not persuade schools to over-react and seek more statemented provision appears to be an impossible task' (p. 149).

It is certainly possible that increased competition between schools will influence the status which is attached to meeting special needs. In some schools there may well be anxiety that devoting time and resources to helping pupils with difficulties will not be as productive as similar investment in raising levels of performance at the opposite end of the ability spectrum. Decisions about staffing could also reflect perceptions of relative value in producing a more scholastic school profile for attracting more customers.

With grant-maintained schools permitted to change their status, any return to a selective system is likely to encourage the view that children with problems can best be helped outside the mainstream of educational provision. This view will be further supported by the extension of local management to special schools (LMSS). Although their funding formula will be based on the notional number of places required rather than the actual number of pupils attending them, special schools will have a clearly vested interest in gaining and retaining a reputation for dealing with youngsters not easily accommodated in the normal school system. This will almost inevitably lead to an emphasis once again on formal assessment and registration at odds with the more informal approaches encouraged over the last decade. As Hope (1989) implies, under LMSS it will be difficult for special schools to resist 'pressures towards isolation or rivalry' (p. 168).

Again management issues can be considered in relation to LEA administration, mainstream and special school policy.

1 Administrators might examine the ways in which account is taken of special needs in devising systems for funding schools and supporting individuals.
2 Primary and secondary schools might assess how far the interests of pupils with special needs are being protected as changes are made in timetables and staffing structures to accommodate the National Curriculum and respond to local management and open enrolment.
3 Special schools might consider whether the demonstration of their willingness and ability to teach the National Curriculum is

compatible with their previous rationale as providers of a more flexible, modified or developmental curriculum.

Tackling these issues will be assisted by some of the more positive elements of curriculum reform.

POSITIVE ELEMENTS OF CURRICULUM REFORM

Against the background of considerable alarm, if not despondency, described above, it is important to maintain a clear perception that there are also some positive aspects of recent reforms which can help planning for provision for special education. Perhaps the most positive elements are best illustrated by the advice forthcoming from the National Curriculum Council in its document *A Curriculum for All* (NCC, 1989).

This publication identifies four elements of school policy and practice which should be considered in plans for ensuring access for pupils with special educational needs to a broad and balanced curriculum. Each school is required to produce a *curriculum development plan* which identifies priorities, targets and resources for organisational change and there will be opportunities here to urge attention to the importance of preparation for teaching groups with a diversity of levels of ability and attainment. *Schemes of work* which are written definitions of work to be done in subject areas over a specific period of time provide another opportunity for ensuring that differentiation to meet a wide range of learning needs becomes an integral part of planning for each area of the curriculum. The *learning environment* should offer extra stimulus and encouragement for overcoming learning difficulties. The identification of *pupils' teaching needs* should lead to detailed plans for individuals with difficulties and disabilities.

If these elements are taken into account then most schools will be much nearer to establishing a whole school policy for meeting special needs than has been the case in the past. However, the effective implementation of such a policy requires continuing and regular review. Too often a whole school policy may represent little more than a statement of intentional goodwill rather than actual practice. There should be a clear delineation of responsibilities within the school organisation for monitoring provision for pupils with special educational needs together with advice, guidance and support for individual classroom management.

Management issues in this context relate to ensuring that the useful processes suggested above are translated into practical action.

1 Administrators might check what happens to school development plans to see that they do not simply become a bureaucratic comforter which offers reassurance that thought has been given to children with special needs. What is done through in-service training to help the differentiation of learning experiences for pupils of diverse abilities?
2 Primary and secondary schools might examine how responsibilities are defined for ensuring that pupils with special needs receive appropriate support and consideration in curriculum planning. How is the learning environment designed, and methods and materials adapted, to meet a diversity of abilities and aptitudes?
3 Special schools might give particular thought to what is different about the nature of their schemes of work and how they complement or improve upon what is offered in the mainstream.

Careful monitoring is essential to the success of development plans and responsibility for this spreads beyond the more immediate professional involvement of teachers and advisors to school governors and the local community.

MONITORING PROVISION

School governors have the legal responsibility for ensuring that identified special needs are being met within a school. It is their duty to see that the school is in fact making necessary arrangements to meet the requirements of formal statements and discovering those children who give 'cause for concern'. In practice the headteacher or a designated member of staff will co-ordinate the combination of support teaching, record keeping and programme planning involved in meeting special needs but particularly with the new responsibilities of local management, governors will be expected to ascertain that appropriate provision is in fact being made.

It is usual nowadays to think in terms of meeting special needs as a *whole school policy*. If indeed the whole school is to be engaged in developing a policy, it should start with a critical look at resources, grouping, timetabling, staffing and the present use of people, buildings and equipment. All too often, instead of this institutional review leading as a *consequence* to the establishment of a corporate policy on special needs, it has been left to individual support teachers or special needs co-ordinators to act as a *catalyst*, stimulating and precipitating change through personal charisma and goodwill.

In order to monitor the system so that undue dependence on individuals is avoided it is necessary to ensure that there is a secure place within the senior management structure and a permanent item on the senior management agenda, for special education. As schools have adapted to local management, many have delegated particular aspects of school governance to sub-committees of senior teachers and governors dealing with detailed administration of finance, buildings, equipment, curriculum and pastoral care. Whatever the specific duties with which such groups are charged, any plans for change should always be scrutinised for their implications for pupils with special educational needs. This might itself be part of a wider brief related to whole school policies for other aspects of equal opportunities such as multi-cultural or gender issues.

In this area illustrative examples of issues which ought to be addressed include:

1   How can administrators ensure that schools are able to undertake a critical review of resources with a view to long-term planning for aspects of policy such as special needs when thoughts of governing bodies may be more urgently concerned with balancing an annual budget subject to a fluctuating formula?

2   How can primary and secondary schools ensure that special needs co-ordination has a senior status within a management structure in which higher salaries may be more easily commanded by subject specialists whose recruitment and retention is essential to maintaining the provision of core and foundation areas in the National Curriculum?

3   How will special schools monitor their role within an integrated system working in partnership not competition with ordinary schools? Will it be possible to sustain moves towards more

integrated provision in the face of pressure to ensure funding by a willingness to recruit and retain pupils?

The successful resolution of managerial issues related to whole school policy on special needs crucially depends on monitoring the effectiveness of two aspects of school organisation: classroom management and access to expert support.

Classroom management

A policy for helping teachers successfully to provide for the special educational needs of individual pupils is not something different from the school's general policies for classroom management, discipline and pastoral care. It is rather a matter of increased awareness that for certain pupils there are particular impediments to social attachment and educational progress which require a special response from teachers (Wehlage *et al.*, 1989).

While the celebration of success is a worthy part of any school development plan, too narrow an interpretation of this goal can lead to problems with low attainers if academic achievement is seen as the only source of success and esteem. Developing a school as a community which values all of its members involves planning suitable learning experiences and conveying positive expectations. Social attachment or a sense of membership and belonging presents problems for pupils who find it difficult to demonstrate academic competence, to meet behavioural expectations or to interact comfortably with adults. Inefficient teaching fails to match learning tasks to pupil ability and leads to frustration and disaffection. An apparent lack of relevance of learning experiences can also lead through boredom to behaviour problems but such friction is avoided by schools which promote an incorporative approach through curriculum planning and personal attention and interest.

Educational progress for children with difficulties is encouraged by developing more co-operative, shared, practical approaches to learning but these are precisely the most difficult methods to use successfully and certainly the most fraught with opportunities for misbehaviour. It is important, therefore, that lesson organisation is carefully analysed in respect of rules, relationships and routines, classroom design and layout, group work and providing support (Smith, 1990).

The special response from teachers which facilitates the social attachment and educational progress of pupils with special educational needs is characterised by acceptance of responsibility, an extended perception of their role as teachers, persistence and optimism (Wehlage *et al.*, 1989). This means a readiness to be accountable for the academic success or improved social and personal competence of pupils who cannot easily make progress on their own. An extended teaching role is one which goes beyond instruction to counselling and friendly contact which penetrates the defensive shell which youngsters with problems may hide behind. Persistence with non-ideal students requires tolerance and an ability to be less quickly offended by undesirable behaviour which may be an expression of accumulated frustration. Optimism means remaining confident in the belief that, however intransigent their difficulties, pupils with special needs have a potential for learning which can be released by skilled teaching.

Access to support

Whatever the undoubted merits of the view that, ultimately, permeation of approaches such as those described above will ensure that all teachers see themselves as teachers of children with special needs, it is important that support is available for attaining that goal. The term *special education* describes a body of knowledge and experience concerning the identification, diagnosis and remediation of learning problems which it is unreasonable to expect that every class teacher or subject specialist will acquire. Each school should therefore have some members of staff who are able to advise colleagues, act as consultants on methods and materials and know where to find additional help outside the school.

To an extent remedial teachers traditionally fulfilled this role in mainstream schools but more recently these wider aspects of the job have been acknowledged by the increased use of the description 'support teaching' to describe the work of the special educator. This has combined the advisory or consultant role with collaborative work alongside colleagues in their classrooms. This role has also extended to being the school's main contact with outside agencies involved in helping children with special needs.

External agents who may be involved include local authority educational support services such as advisers, inspectors and in most authorities a team of peripatetic support teachers able to give schools extra assistance with individual pupils or more general aspects of special needs work in developing policies and in-service training. In recent years many special schools have sought to provide support through *outreach* teaching in local mainstream schools. Other agencies include educational psychologists, social workers, doctors and other health workers. Keeping contact with this vast range of personnel requires clear and effective channels for communication, information and review and referral. Equally, if not more important are the similar requirements for liaison with parents who are essential partners in the process of education as participants in assessment and teaching.

If special education is to continue to be taken seriously as an essential part of the normal educational system and there is both a legal obligation and a philosophical commitment for this to happen, then to make sure that reality matches the rhetoric, the management of special needs must be a clearly defined responsibility at national, local authority and school level. There is a danger that a laudable attempt to refrain from labelling and stereotyping handicapped children may provide an excuse for ignoring problems or pretending that they do not exist. Mainstream schools may be tempted to avoid tackling problems which appear to present an inordinate drain on limited resources and special schools may be tempted to revert to a role as caring havens for those pupils unwanted by the mainstream.

Describing needs and defining the resources required to meet them should not mean labelling individuals or simply defending vested professional interests. There are some dangers that this is precisely what may be encouraged by recent reforms but approaches to the management of special needs which effectively identify and tackle relevant issues will continue to maintain the protective but progressive role of special education.

REFERENCES

Booth, T., Potts, P. and Swann, W. (eds) (1987) *Preventing Difficulties in Learning: Curriculum for All,* London: Blackwell.

Brennan, W.K. (1987) *Changing Special Education Now*, Milton Keynes: Open University Press.

Caldwell, P. (1989) 'The Education Act 1981', in T. Bowers (ed.) *Managing Special Needs*, Milton Keynes: Open University Press.

DES (1978) *Special Educational Needs* (The Warnock Report), London: HMSO.

——(1983) *Circular 1/83: Assessments and Statements of Special Educational Needs.*

——(1989) *Circular 22/89: Assessments and Statements of Special Educational Needs Procedures within the Educational, Health and Social Services.*

Fish, J. (1989) *What is Special Education?*, Milton Keynes: Open University Press.

Goacher, B., Evans, J., Welton, J. and Wedell, K. (1988) *Policy and Provision for Special Educational Needs: Implementing the 1981 Education Act*, London: Cassell.

Gross, H. and Gipps, C. (1987) *Supporting Warnock's Eighteen Percent: Six Case Studies*, Lewes: Falmer Press.

Hope, M. (1989) 'The introduction of the National Curriculum: implications for management in special schools', in T. Bowers (ed.) *Managing Special Needs*, Milton Keynes: Open University Press.

NCC (1989) *Curriculum Guidance Two: A Curriculum for All: Special Needs in the National Curriculum*, York: National Curriculum Council.

Smith, C.J. (1990) 'Analysing classroom organisation', in M. Scherer, I. Gersch and C. Fry (eds) *Meeting Disruptive Behaviour – Assessment, Intervention and Partnership*, London: Macmillan.

Wehlage, G.G., Rutter, R.A., Smith, G.A., Lesko, N. and Fernandez, R.R. (1989) *Reducing the Risk: Schools as Communities of Support*, Lewes: Falmer Press.

3

LEARNING DIFFICULTIES

Ronald Gulliford

The most frequent sources of special educational needs are difficulties in learning which, in various degrees, hinder the development of literacy and numeracy skills needed in other areas of the curriculum. The sources of such difficulties may include slow cognitive development (reasoning, problem solving, remembering and generalising) and slow language development. However, some children of average or even superior abilities may have marked difficulties in acquiring reading and writing skills. Emotional and adjustment difficulties may contribute to learning difficulties, sometimes as a result of unsettled home circumstances, sometimes as a consequence of feelings of failure. Mild sensory disabilities, speech and language difficulties, health problems resulting in absences, irregular attendance for other reasons are frequently additional factors.

The degree of learning difficulty is also influenced by school factors: the recognition of individual needs and the degree of personal support which is given by individual teachers; the setting of appropriate expectations for learning and the provision of methods of teaching suited to slower learners (appropriate content and language); the planned teaching of important concepts and skills; providing motivation by suitable but optimistic expectations and especially by ensuring tangible success. In other words, a learning difficulty is to be understood in terms of the interaction of individual pupils' characteristics and needs with the expectations, content and teaching methods of the school.

The Warnock Report (DES, 1978) recommended that children should be viewed in terms of their educational and personal needs rather than their disabilities. Significantly, it was in a chapter with

41

the title 'Some curricular needs' that the Report distinguished and briefly discussed four degrees of learning difficulty: mild, moderate, specific and severe. (The latter are the subject of the next chapter.)

Children with mild learning difficulties were seen as forming the largest group of children requiring some form of additional teaching and personal and educational support in ordinary schools. Moderate learning difficulties were described as stemming from a variety and combination of causes which 'often include mild and multiple physical and sensory disabilities, an impoverished or adverse social or educational background, specific learning difficulties and limited general ability'. They were seen as constituting 'the largest group of children in special schools and a large proportion of children in many ordinary schools for whom special education is needed' (p. 219).

Specific learning difficulties referred to children with severe and long-term difficulties in reading, writing and spelling but whose abilities are at least average and for whom distinctive arrangements are needed.

The size of the problem was shown by a large survey undertaken by Croll and Moses (1985) in the period following the Warnock Report. They selected at random sixty-one junior schools in ten LEAs. Through personal interviews with junior teachers as well as the schools' headteachers, they sought information about the nature, sources and frequency of special needs as well as about methods of assessment, record keeping and special help provided by the school, by school psychological services, remedial teaching and other peripatetic services. Of the 12,310 pupils in the sixty-one schools, 18.8 per cent were considered by teachers as having special needs, 15 per cent as having a learning difficulty, 7.7 per cent presented behaviour problems and 4.5 per cent had either a health problem or a sensory or physical disability. A number of pupils were noted as having learning, behavioural and health problems. There were differences between schools: thirteen nominated 10 per cent or less as having special needs, twenty-six with 10–20 per cent, eighteen with 20–30 per cent and four more than 30 per cent. In first year juniors, 18 per cent were considered to have a learning difficulty, which in the fourth year was only reduced to 13 per cent. Half of those deemed to have special needs received some form of special help either from the schools' resources or from support services. Withdrawal teaching was provided for just under 9 per cent of the total sample, mostly for one or two hours a week and rarely for more than three hours a week. Only three of the schools had a special class, a form of provision not favoured by headteachers.

SUPPORT FOR LEARNING

Remedial teaching services have increasingly seen their role as providing support to teachers and pupils within schools and classes rather than by periods of withdrawal to a remedial centre or class. In an evaluation of one authority's remedial support services, Richmond and Smith (1990) interviewed forty-two primary teachers for their views about the different kinds of support they needed or received. During the two years of the study, two-thirds had talked with visiting remedial teachers or advisers or with other specialist staff such as educational psychologists. They valued such opportunities for seeing a child's problems from a new angle and often for reassurance that they were doing the right things. As one teacher said, 'professional support is almost pastoral support' (p. 300). A view often expressed was that other professionals should 'become part of us, part of the school' (p. 301) – meaning that they would get to know the children and the teachers' problems better in relation to giving advice on teaching methods and materials. They approved of the visiting teacher working with them in the classroom but at the same time they were in favour of withdrawal teaching for some children because it allowed for more individual attention and provided a good working environment away from the bustle of the classroom. They stressed the need for liaison and for coordination of the remedial teacher's and class teacher's role.

Poor achievements in literacy skills are a handicap across the curriculum. Until the late 1970s, the problem in secondary schools was seen as a job for the remedial department in a context which still included streaming and withdrawal for remedial teaching. Golby and Gulliver (1979) argued for an extended role for the remedial teacher, contributing to educational change by being supportive to the pupil and subject teacher in assisting access to the curriculum. In the 1980s, schools began to move towards a system in which remedial teachers and others gave support across the curriculum within classes which included several pupils with special needs. This approach has been an important element within 'whole school policies for special needs'.

The experiences of a number of schools in developing a whole school approach have been the subject of journal articles; a useful collection has been compiled by Ainscow and Florek (1989). Garnett (1976) described how moving a secondary school unit for pupils with moderate learning difficulties from the periphery to the centre of the school led to the pupils' increased participation in ordinary classes and also to a change in the remedial teacher's role. This developed into support and advice to mainstream teachers and a system of key or liaison teachers nominated in each department. The remedial teacher's role came to include that of a coordinator for special needs (Garnett, 1983).

In another comprehensive school, which had a traditional pattern of withdrawal for remedial teaching, a proposal for the development of a whole school approach was discussed for a whole year by a working party consisting of senior staff and representatives of each department, the latter keeping other colleagues informed (Giles and Dunlop, 1986). Finally, the proposed pattern for supporting pupils in ordinary classes was explained to, and discussed by, the whole staff, which voted in favour of the proposal. Its implementation involved a programme of in-service training for those undertaking support teaching and for the key teachers responsible for liaison with the coordinator and with colleagues in their own departments. A wide range of issues was covered such as adapting curriculum materials, the role of various support services and specialised spelling lists for subject areas. The 'remedial image' in the minds of both pupils and staff was changed by the coordinator's move from the former remedial room on the periphery of the school to a central position and by the development of a different set of roles, working through the key teachers and acting as the channel to outside agencies such as advisory and support services and social services.

Willey (1989) discussed the development of a whole school approach in a primary school. Whereas one might think that the absence of departmental structures would make it easier to develop a common policy, her experience suggests that individual views are not held lightly and need the opportunity for expression and tactful consideration. She suggests starting with a topic in an area about which there is already some agreement and about which some collecting of information or observation can be a practical starting point. Once one project is underway the possibility of others to follow can be planned over a period of three or four years.

However, there is some way to go before whole school policies are widely adopted and procedures are developed. An HMI Survey of provision for special needs in top primary and first-year secondary schools (DES, 1989) noted that half the schools had reviewed their identification and monitoring procedures, classroom practice and staff training for pupils with special needs. In almost all of these, a whole school policy had been adopted. Nevertheless, three-quarters of the schools withdrew pupils at times for an often limited range of language and computational skills, frequently unrelated to their mainstream work. But support teaching within mainstream classes was a growing practice and was judged effective when there was agreement about how collaboration was planned, monitored and recorded.

The desirable elements of an agreement about methods of collaboration have been the subject of a number of studies by Thomas (1986; Thomas and Jackson, 1986). In a secondary school setting, he pointed to the difficulty of providing for the special needs of individuals at the same time as managing the rest of the class and he proposed two distinct roles: someone working with individual children for short periods of time, say, from four to fifteen minutes, working on a rota of pupils and having prepared materials to work from. The second role is someone concentrating on the class as a whole, circulating quickly and providing pupils with feedback on work and on behaviour.

Another form of support has developed between special and ordinary schools. An educational psychologist and the headteacher of a special school for children with moderate difficulties argued in an influential article that too much emphasis had been placed on the identification of children for special schooling and too little on examining constructive ways of supporting the efforts of classroom teachers and parents before a crisis has been reached (Hallmark and Dessent, 1983). They described how one girl had been referred with a view to special school placement because of lack of progress and continual and persistent demands on the teacher's time. However, an input by a teacher from a nearby special school was provided for one afternoon a week. His task was to identify what learning materials were required to meet her needs. The work to be achieved during the next week was decided and agreed with the class teacher; appropriate resources – worksheets, number games, etc. – were provided. The result was that the child made progress and ultimately was no longer regarded as needing special school placement. This 'outreach' support was subsequently provided on a weekly basis to other schools in the area. The scheme has now been operating for over a decade; its development has been described by Smith and Keogh (1990).

Links of this and other kinds between special and ordinary schools increased rapidly in the mid-1980s. An NFER survey in a quarter of LEAs (Jowett *et al.*, 1987) reported finding 197 special schools involved in links with ordinary schools, another 26 were planning to do so and five had previously had them. Some 1,600 pupils were involved, mainly special school pupils going into the ordinary school for particular curriculum activities. A third of special schools in the survey had staff going out to ordinary schools for varying amounts of time, a quarter for at least one full day. Their activities, in order of frequency, were: teaching mixed classes of mainstream and special school pupils, advising mainstream colleagues and supporting pupils from the special school. An enquiry by Day (1989) over an extensive area provided an informed and balanced appraisal of outreach in which he identified four models (exporting the behavioural objectives approach; resource delivery, consultancy and partnership) as well as the different issues at primary and secondary levels as outreach moved from a pioneering stage to one involving LEA coordination.

PARENTS HELP READING

A successful development in recent years has been the involvement of parents in helping their children's reading. There must be many parents who, anxious about their children's difficulties or limited progress, have attempted to help at home. Hewison's finding that children who read to their parents on a regular basis obtained higher reading scores led on to the Haringey project (Tizard *et al.*, 1982), which was organised so that every child in two randomly chosen top infant classes in two schools in an inner city multi-racial area were heard daily by their parents, reading books sent home by their teachers. Parents welcomed the project and also the twice-termly visits of one of the researchers. The parents' role was to listen to their children's reading rather than to teach. The results at the end of the two-year project showed a significant improvement by children who received extra practice at home. Three years after the project, Hewison reported that 60 per cent of the project children were reading at or above the average for their age compared with less than 40 per cent of the control children.

A more active role for parents (or some other 'helper') is given in 'paired reading', which was first described by Morgan (1976). A recent evaluation was made by Morgan and Gavin (1988). He had been helping a child with a severe stammer to improve his speech fluency by reading together (simultaneous reading) from a book chosen to suit the pupil's maturity and interest level. He noticed that the procedure was also improving reading skills. Among the features of paired reading he suggests: the child's free choice of reading material, including that which may be above current reading skill but appropriate to the pupil's age and interest; positive reinforcement; giving help four seconds after the child gets stuck on a word; and encouraging the use of context. The method has been widely used by remedial and school psychological services (Topping and Wolfendale, 1985).

Another study involving parents in using the method of paired reading was described by Young and Tyre (1983). Thirteen children who had been independently diagnosed as dyslexic were matched closely with thirty children nominated by schools as severely retarded in reading. Half of these formed a matched group to be given reading help; the other half formed a control group. The parents of children in the first two groups gave children thirty minutes' help every day for a year and allowed their children to attend three Holiday Schools for a week in each of three holiday periods. The parents were given clear guide-lines for helping their children as well as familiarising them with the materials and activities they would be using. A teacher-researcher also visited them regularly. At the end of the year, the children in the two taught groups had made between one to three years' improvement. Only two of the controls had made as much as one year; nine made only six months' gain.

An important issue in helping children as they read is how we should help when they make a mistake or cannot read a word. Glyn (1980) observed that parents tended to give the word immediately.

Moreover, they supplied the correct word more often than they provided prompts and they used praise extremely rarely. In involving parents he therefore advised the following tutoring behaviours: first, praise for reading a sentence correctly; praise for a self-correction; praise for a correct word after a prompt. Second, when a word presents a problem, sufficient time is given for an attempt. If there is no response or there is an incorrect one, the reader is prompted with clues about the meaning of the story or with clues about the way the word looks. If these are not successful, the child should read on to the end of the sentence or read again from the beginning of the sentence, hopefully to use context clues. If these prompts are not successful, the word should be supplied.

A remedial strategy based on this and called 'Pause, Prompt and Praise' was described by Wheldall *et al.*, (1987). The essence of the approach is that a tutor (teacher, parent, an older pupil) provides appropriate feedback as a child reads, i.e. when the child makes an error or hesitates, the tutor pauses for at least five seconds to give the reader the opportunity to self-correct or to work out the word independently. If no response is made, the tutor then prompts, for example, giving cues about the meaning or the context. If the miscue fits the context but is incorrect, the tutor prompts the reader to check the letters or syllables of the word or to re-read from the beginning of the sentence or further into the sentence for contextual cues. If the word is not identified from one or two prompts the word is supplied. The article reported comparisons between tutors trained in this way with tutors not trained; the latter rarely delayed before supplying the word. In a separate enquiry, recordings were made of teachers listening to children reading. It was found that only about 20 per cent of teachers' responses were delayed more than five seconds. Giving parents, or other helpers, a procedure to follow seems desirable.

TWO IMPORTANT SKILLS

Poor spelling is commonly linked with poor reading but may also occur with good readers – and is often associated with poor writing. Pupils with spelling difficulties should be given a technique for learning spellings or in correcting mistakes in written work. Peters (1967) advocated the procedure of Look, Cover, Write, Check – i.e. for learning new or misspelt words, the child looks at the word carefully, pronouncing its syllables; the child covers the word and writes it from memory; checks the spelling and if it is correct the procedure is repeated three times, i.e. to promote 'over-learning'. If incorrect, the cover–write–check procedure should be repeated until correct. In the Fernald kinaesthetic method, the teacher pronounces the word and writes it in large letters; the child repeats the word and traces over it several times with a finger, pronouncing the syllables in doing so. The child writes the word from memory and checks it. If incorrect the procedure is repeated until successful. Probably its main effect is through ensuring attention to the sounds of the word and their representation in the letters and spelling patterns of the word as it is written.

The development of an efficient writing style is desirable for all pupils but a particular attention to handwriting is needed with children who have learning difficulties and those who are left-handers or have uncertain laterality. It is important to teach the formation of letters and how they are joined and to ensure early correction of inappropriate ones. It is also important to give guided practice to ensure correct positioning of the paper and the way of holding the writing instrument. This is particularly important in the case of left-handed pupils. There are now several authoritative books and other teaching materials available. These include guidance for left-handers and for poor writing in the secondary age groups. It is desirable to notice those whose letter formations and joins (or idiosyncratic hold of the pen or pencil) are an impediment to speedy and readable writing; there is now plenty of good advice available (Alston and Taylor, 1988; Sassoon, 1983).

SPECIFIC LEARNING DIFFICULTIES

The Warnock Committee received much evidence from dyslexia associations about children of average or above average abilities who had marked difficulties in learning to read, write and spell. Although they considered that there were no agreed criteria for distinguishing such children, they accepted that there are children whose reading abilities are significantly below the standards which their abilities in other directions would lead one to expect. At the time of this report, a number of independent centres, clinics or schools for teaching dyslexic children had been in existence for some time. An account of their methods by Naidoo (1981) indicated similarities in their remedial methods: they all emphasised phonic work from the beginning, matching and associating the sounds of spoken language with their symbols in written language, starting with the smallest sound symbol unit and proceeding to build words. Miles (1983) emphasised that teaching approaches need to be structured, sequential, cumulative and multi-sensory. His methods involved the progressive and systematic building up of knowledge and skills in recognising and using common letter patterns within words: single letters, digraphs, blends and the more familiar prefixes and suffixes, recognising them in print and associating them with the sound in the spoken word. Most schemes for teaching dyslexic children have put an emphasis on trying to ensure the learning of this relationship.

A booklet by an LEA advisory teacher, who also had experience of teaching in a centre for dyslexic children, provides a practical introduction to teaching methods based on primary methods, drawing upon children's interests and story-books (Cotterell, 1985). It includes for the teacher's use a check-list of basic sounds and their representation in written words; examples of ways of teaching blending; the use of the Fernald kinaesthetic method. To assist the teaching of the link between speech and symbol the Edith Norrie letter-case is described. The latter is a box with partitions in which letters are arranged according to the way letter-sounds are produced: lip sounds in the left-hand sections, tip of the tongue sounds in the middle ones and sounds produced at the back of the throat in a right-hand one. Vowel sounds are represented by red letters placed at the front of the box. After a sentence has been put together, it is read back by the pupil and then written from memory in a topic book. The process develops the child's awareness of the sounds within words and links the sounds with the letters and combinations of letters for representing them. The process of writing them further promotes the learning.

The variety of hypotheses about the nature and sources of specific reading difficulties is considerable. In recent years, researchers in cognitive psychology have been interested in the problem. Several recent books have been written in a style which communicates to the ordinary reader (e.g. Snowling, 1987; Bryant and Bradley, 1985). Snowling suggests that the predominant view is that dyslexia is associated with phonological difficulties originating within spoken language processes – specifically, a weakness or deficiency in phoneme segmentation, i.e. discriminating the sounds of spoken words on which depends the ability to associate them with the spelling patterns in written words. There are other factors varying with individuals, for example, in the ability to discriminate the spelling patterns in print or writing. Other variables are the child's vocabulary and understanding of the meanings of words, phrases and sentences. Snowling hypothesises that there is also a sub-group of dyslexic children who are developmentally delayed, the sources of which could be genetic, environmental or emotional. Although not reading at the expected time, their phonological difficulties are mild. How well they develop is likely to depend on there being no disparity between visual perceptual ability, semantic understanding and phonological skills. In teaching them, of particular importance are ensuring the links between sounds and their representation in print as well as ensuring that the content and contexts of reading are meaningful.

Another publication (Bryant and Bradley, 1985) gives a very readable account of issues and findings from several years of research. They suggest that any successful way of teaching children with specific reading difficulties should:

1 foster children's awareness of sounds within words;
2 show them how to make generalisations about spelling;
3 emphasise and demonstrate the connection between reading and spelling and between the phonological and visual aspects of reading; and
4 cater for the fact that different backward readers may set about reading in different ways.

Their experiments indicated the benefits of two of their methods. The first aimed at improving phonological skills by using plastic letters to make words so that children became more aware of the sounds shared by different words and that words with common sounds often share the same spelling pattern. The second method is based on the Fernald method which has already been described.

Reason (1990) has discussed the question whether teaching children with specific reading difficulties requires distinctive methods or whether the difficulties can be circumvented by enhanced opportunities for natural language-based reading experiences. She argues that there can be no certain recipe for teaching children with specific reading difficulties and that, while traditional definitions focus on the recognition and reproduction of print, other aspects of literacy development should not be ignored, i.e. the context of learning (the child's experiences; expectations of enjoyment and competence; effort after meaning; shared knowledge) as well as language learning and its purpose of communication. While some children need to learn in a very precise way, it should be in the context of a rich and enjoyable experience of language and communication. This is a helpful conclusion since it encourages the teacher to be informed about – and alert to – the kinds of difficulty which may be holding the child back and which may indicate a particular emphasis in giving help, but it also confirms the importance of the rich language and other experiences of the primary classroom (Reason *et al.*, 1988; Reason, 1990).

It is worth noting that there are other specific difficulties which should be considered. One is that of the 'clumsy child', also termed 'perceptuo-motor dysfunction'. There seems to be a renewed interest in this, judging by a number of recent articles in *Support for Learning* in 1987 and 1988. Difficulties may be manifest in physical education, throwing, catching, balancing, dressing, writing and other practical tasks. Consequences can be social, e.g. non-participation in ball games on the playground and lack of friends. Laszlo *et al.* (1988) report on a study which obtained positive effects from a training programme. An article by Venables (1988) described and evaluated a week's intensive holiday course for a group of children identified as having the disability. The activities included practice in certain skills such as dressing, balancing, climbing, throwing, handwriting, articulation. A Lecturer in Movement has outlined some remedial measures within school activities such as movement, dance, gymnastics and swimming (Price, 1989).

AREAS OF THE CURRICULUM

Children with learning difficulties have often experienced a limited curriculum partly as a result of separate forms of provision and partly because their difficulties were deemed to need a modified curriculum. In recent years, there has been a steady increase in publications referring to curricular issues and teaching methods. The National Curriculum has been seen as a challenge and an opportunity.

Primary school provision for special needs in relation to the National Curriculum is given a detailed and insightful examination by Ann Lewis (1991). She sees the National Curriculum as having potential benefits such as making it more likely that children with learning difficulties will be taught in mainstream classes with their peers and be working on the common curriculum. Referring to the fact that many primary schools now have a designated teacher for special needs, she emphasises the importance of recognising that special needs remains a collective responsibility. One concern she expresses refers to the possibility that such children might be given more work directed to core subjects and less on other areas – which would be counter-productive since broad integrated work may well provide a basis for children learning to apply and generalise skills and knowledge and will also maximise motivation. Further chapters consider forms of help in gaining access to the National Curriculum: the planning of intermediate goals, i.e. analysis of the task and of the teacher's role; matching topics with children's interest levels; varying the presentation of the activity to suit individual needs; methods of grouping; the important issues of resources, record keeping and assessment. In a chapter on safeguarding the curriculum, she devotes seven pages to an examination of the very relevant issue of time: stated time allocation in National Curriculum documents; the question of how additional curricular requirements can be fitted into the timetable; increasing the time available for teaching/learning; using classroom time more effectively.

Policy into practice in the core National Curriculum at primary level is discussed in a book by Coulby and Ward (1990). They suggest that of the three core subjects in the National Curriculum, science is likely to need most changes to practice in primary schools: finding more time for it; planning work within a defined framework and developing an investigative approach. They refer to the danger that some teachers may adopt a curriculum led by attainment targets and that this can be avoided, as the non-statutory guidance suggests, by using the programmes of study. Like Lewis, they see the need for integrated activities in view of time constraints. For example, they describe a project to redecorate and refurbish a 'quiet room' area in the open-plan classroom, which became the subject of a cross-curricular approach to the three core subjects of the National Curriculum. In fact, forty-one activities during the project could be related to attainment targets at levels three to six: nineteen in

English, ten in Maths and twelve in science. A chapter on science describes how two teachers in different schools prepared themselves for the role of science coordinator and how they developed their science curriculum related to National Curriculum targets.

Practical projects comparable to the redecoration of 'the quiet room' mentioned above have often provided experiences for pupils with learning difficulties, especially perhaps in special schools. In a discussion of 'Mathematics in transition', Williams (1990) stresses how important it is to give thought to 'identifying the opportunities for developing mathematics out of cross-curricular work' or what can be achieved through the pupils' own experiences in the environment or life of the school. He suggests that the collective need of a group activity is 'likely to engender confidence, motivation and ability to deal mathematically with real life situations which can subsequently be applied to many survival skills required in later life'. However, he wisely comments that, unlike the tidy problems presented by teachers and textbooks, real life mathematics can bring up unexpected problems and 'a modicum of pre-planning may not only cut down the time the teacher needs to spend on dealing with individual difficulties but can also help to achieve the ordered progression which the National Curriculum demands'. From long experience in teaching mathematics with pupils with moderate learning difficulties, he makes very pertinent comments on issues in teaching mathematics in the National Curriculum.

'History in primary schools' (Blyth 1989) is rich in ideas and resources for teaching history 5 to 11 and would be very useful in developing programmes meeting National Curriculum proposals for history. The content includes the planning of schemes of work and activities at the infant and junior stages. A chapter on 'the classroom operation' is concerned with the variety of activities which can be employed according to need, e.g. the story lesson, interpreting illustrations, exposition and questions, making records, field work, art work, model making and visual displays, time lines. Further chapters consider: first, sources and resources; and second, methods of assessment, evaluation and record keeping. An example of a resource for time lines is Timeline (West, 1986), a structured history scheme which aims to organise children's ideas about the past through the use of thirty-two cards, each with ten pictures concerned with a major historical theme or concept from caveman to the present. Each card asks a question about time and evidence which children explore through group discussion and individual follow-up work. Being picture-based, it can be used to develop history skills at any age or ability level from seven to thirteen. A popular resource in schools are the history series on educational TV such as 'History Around You' (Granada) and 'How We Used to Live' (Yorkshire TV), although Blyth comments that the excellence of the programmes tempts teachers to rely too heavily upon them; it is hoped that the National Curriculum will guide schools in constructing their own schemes of work to use such programmes as tools.

In the last ten years or so, articles, pamphlets and books on the teaching of history to low attainers of secondary age have been written by history teachers. While their suggestions about content may need to be matched with National Curriculum requirements, their suggestions for topics and methods are valid and useful. A thirty-page pamphlet written for the Historical Association (Cowie, 1980) refers first to the aims, benefits and potential difficulties in teaching history and goes on to provide useful suggestions and comments on oral work, the use of books, visual materials, TV and radio, written work, simulations and games, field work and museums, the use of maps and local resources whether in town or country. Consideration is given to different approaches: lines of development in topics (such as homes, transport, costume, warfare) which have the benefit of chronological sequence; local history studies drawing upon the evidence of change in the nearby environment; family history including comparing the present with when grandparents were young; and the use of historical fiction. Another publication from the same source offers further guidance (Hodgkinson, 1982).

A useful publication for secondary teaching was based on a Northern Ireland summer school which brought together history teachers and special needs staff and was followed up in groups over two years. The resulting publication covers twelve topics including, for example, design and use of worksheets, history trails, local history studies, the use of micros and a survey of resources (McIver, 1982).

Wilson (1985) discussed, in some detail, teaching methods and resources in teaching history with slow learners: language and communication; readability of texts and materials; the use of different kinds of written work – description, recording, expressive and imaginative writing; establishing a key vocabulary; sequencing exercises, e.g. describing an historical event; creative writing; talk and discussion. A useful chapter discusses materials aiding learning: visual materials; diagrams, primary source material and artefacts; games, simulations, role play and drama. No doubt most specialist teachers of history will know of these publications; support teachers would also find them useful in understanding their support role.

A number of publications by the Geographical Association refer to themes and teaching approaches from the infant reception class through to the secondary age groups. A booklet on geography at primary and middle school level (Mills, 1981) includes an account of activities for infants which introduced words relating to position and location (up, down, over, under, beside, next to, behind) and approaches to mapwork (e.g. simple plans) and topic work (homes, transport and, with 7-year-olds, pollution). A booklet edited by Boardman (1982) has contributions from secondary teachers of slow learners on weather, the seasons, developing mapping skills, road networks, basic ideas in agriculture and settlement. He also describes a method for developing the concept of a map as a plan: children construct cardboard models of buildings and place them on a hardboard base covered with paper. They draw round the base of each building, remove the models and see that what is left is a map. Then each side of the map is divided into equal units; lines are drawn across, creating squares which are numbered on one side and lettered on the other. They then practise giving the location of buildings in terms of letters and numbers. Another concept, that of the representation of height on a map by contour lines, is tackled by making a model of an island. This is placed in a transparent tank, the side of which is marked with a vertical scale graduated at regular intervals. Water is poured in until it reaches the first point of the scale and the 'sea level' is marked on the island. The water level is brought up to the next level which is marked round the island. The process is repeated several times and the children observe that contour lines are drawn on the mountain at regular intervals. The process is taken a step further: a sheet of acetate is placed across the top of the tank and the contour lines on the model are copied on to the acetate with a fibre tip pen. In other words the pupils have seen a model transferred into a map. Other contributors to the publication describe other ways of developing geographical concepts in practical and interesting ways. In another publication, Williams (1982) discusses the development at primary and secondary age groups of graphicacy, i.e. the skills required in reading, interpreting and drawing maps and diagrams, and relating photographs and maps of an area. He explains the difficulties and indicates a number of sources on the topic. (Recent publications are obtainable from the Geographical Association, 343 Fulwood Road, Sheffield, S10 3BP.)

REFERENCES

Ainscow, M. and Florek, A. (eds) (1989) *Special Educational Needs: Towards a Whole School Approach,* London: David Fulton.

Alston, J. (1988) *The Handwriting File,* Wisbech: Learning Development Aids.

Blyth, J. (1989) *History in Primary Schools,* Milton Keynes: Open University Press.

Boardman, D. (ed.) (1982) *Geography for Slow Learners,* Sheffield: The Geographical Association.

Bryant, P. and Bradley, L. (1985) *Children's Reading Problems,* Oxford: Basil Blackwell.

Cotterell, G. (1985) *Teaching the Non-reading Dyslexic Child,* Wisbech: Learning Development Aids.

Coulby, D. and Ward, S. (1990) *The Primary Core National Curriculum,* London: Cassell.

Cowie, E.E. (1979) *History and the Slow Learning Child,* London: The Historical Association.

Croll, P. and Moses, D. (1985) *One In Five: the assessment and incidence of special educational needs,* London: Routledge and Kegan Paul.

Day, A. (1989) 'Reaching out: the background to outreach', in D. Baker and K. Bovair (eds) *Making the Special School Ordinary Vol. One, Models for the Developing Special Schools,* Lewes: Falmer Press.

Department of Education and Science (1978) *Special Educational Needs* (The Warnock Report), London: HMSO.

——(1989) *HMI Report: A survey of Pupils with Special Educational Needs in Ordinary Schools,* London: HMSO.

Fernald, G. (1943) *Remedial Techniques in Basic School Subjects,* New York: McGraw Hill.

Garnett, J. (1976) 'Special children in a comprehensive', *Special Education,* 3, 1, 8–11.

——(1988) 'Support teaching: taking a closer look', *British Journal for Special Education,* 15, 1, 15–18.

Giles, C. and Dunlop, S. (1986) 'Changing direction at Tile Hill Wood', *British Journal of Special Education,* 13, 3, 120–3.

Glyn, T. (1980) 'Parent and child interaction in reading at home', in M.M.

Clark and T. Glyn (eds) 'Reading and writing for the child with difficulties', *Educational Review Occasional Publications*, No. 8.

Golby, M. and Gulliver, R.J. (1979) 'Whose remedies? whose ills?', *Journal of Curriculum Studies*, 11, 137–47.

Hallmark, N. and Dessent, T. (1982) 'A special education service centre', *Special Education*, 9, 1, 6–8.

Jowett, S., Hegarty, S. and Moses, D. (1988) *Joining Forces*, Slough: National Foundation for Educational Research.

Lazlo, J., Bairstow, P. and Bartrip, J. (1988) 'A new approach to treatment of perceptuo-motor dysfunction, previously called clumsiness', *Support for Learning*, 3, 1, 35–40.

Lewis, A. (1981) *Primary Special Needs and the National Curriculum*, London: Routledge.

McIver, V. (ed.) (1982) *Teaching History to Slow Learning Children in Secondary Schools*, Belfast: Stranmillis College.

Miles, T.R. (1983) *Dyslexia: the Pattern of Difficulties*, St Albans: Granada.

Mills, D. (ed.) (1981) *Geographical Work in Primary and Middle Schools*, The Geographical Association.

Morgan, R.T.T. (1976) 'Paired reading tuition: a preliminary report', *Child Care Health and Development*, 2, 13–28.

Morgan, R.T.T. and Gavin, P. (1988) 'Paired reading: evaluation and progress', *Support for Learning*, 3, 4, 201–6.

Naidoo, S. (1981) 'Teaching methods and their rationale', in G.Th. Pavlidis and T.R. Miles (eds) *Dyslexia Research and its Applications to Education*, New York: John Wiley.

Peters, M.L. (1967) *Spelling Caught or Taught*, London: Routledge and Kegan Paul.

Price, D. (1989) 'Low achievers in physical education', in A. Ramasut (ed.) *Whole School Approaches to Special Needs*, Lewes: Falmer Press.

Reason, R. (1990) 'Reconciling different approaches to intervention', in P.D. Pumfrey and C.D. Elliott (eds) *Children's Difficulties in Reading, Spelling and Writing*, Lewes: Falmer Press.

Reason, R., Brown, B., Cole, M. and Gregory, M. (1988) 'Does the "specific" in specific learning difficulties make a difference to the way we teach?', *Support for Learning*, 3, 4, 230–6.

Richmond, R.C. and Smith, C.J. (1990) 'Support for special needs', *Oxford Review of Education*, 16, 3, 295–309.

Sassoon, R. (1983) *The Practical Guide to Children's Handwriting*, London: Thames and Hudson.

Smith, D. and Keogh, P. (1990) 'A decade of support – one school's practice', in D. Baker and K. Bovair, *Making Special Schools Ordinary Vol. 2*, Lewes: Falmer Press.

Snowling, M. (1987) *Dyslexia. A Cognitive Developmental Perspective*, Oxford: Basil Blackwell.

Thomas, G. (1986) 'Integrating personnel in order to integrate children', *Support for Learning*, 1, 1, 19–26.

Thomas, G. and Jackson, B. (1986) 'The whole school approach to integration', *British Journal of Special Education*, 13, 1, 27–9.

Tizard, J., Schofield, W.N. and Hewison. J. (1982) 'Collaboration between teachers and parents in assisting children's reading', *British Journal of Educational Psychology*, 52, 1–15.

Topping, K. and Wolfendale, S. (eds) (1985) *Parents' Involvement in Children's Reading*, London: Croom Helm.

Venables, A. (1988) 'Clumsy children: an account of a week's course', *Support for Learning*, 3, 4, 5–12.

West, J. (1986) *Timeline*, Walton-on-Thames: Thomas Nelson.

Wheldall, K., Merrett, F. and Colmar, S. (1987) 'Pause, prompt and praise for parents and peers: effective tutoring of low progress readers', *Support for Learning*, 2, 1, 5–12.

Willey, M. (1989) 'Moving from policy to practice', in M. Ainscow and A. Florek (eds) (1989) *Special Educational Needs: Towards a Whole School Approach*, London: David Fulton.

Williams, A. (1990) 'Mathematics in transition', *British Journal of Special Education*, 17, 2, 57–60.

Wilson, M.D. (1985) *History for Pupils with Learning Difficulties*, London: Hodder and Stoughton.

Young, P. and Tyre, C. (1983) *Dyslexia or Illiteracy*, Milton Keynes: Open University Press.

4

SEVERE LEARNING DIFFICULTIES

Christina Tilstone

INTRODUCTION

This chapter is concerned with the educational needs of children
with severe learning difficulties, some of whom may have autism
and/or additional physical and sensory impairments. It should be
stressed that children with autism do not necessarily have severe
learning difficulties although Frith (1989) reports that three out of
four autistic children will show evidence of 'mental retardation'.
Severe learning difficulties was the Warnock Report's (DES, 1978)
preferred description of children previously referred to as mentally
handicapped; a term which itself had replaced a number of others
all of which had negative connotations. Before 1971, these children
were excluded from the educational system in Britain and were the
responsibility of the Health service, whether in residential
institutions or living at home and attending one of the training
centres which had been developed during the post-war period. In
1971 they became the responsibility of the Education service and the
training centres became schools. This change was partly the result
of pressure from parents' organisations but other significant factors
in the change were research findings which demonstrated that these
children were by no means incapable of learning. There thus began
a period of development in educational provision, continually
increasing aspirations for the goals of their education and for the
normalisation of their experience and participation in the
community. These developments were further promoted by the
provision of courses of initial and in-service teacher education.

These pupils form part of the 2 per cent of children which the
Warnock Report suggested require highly specialised help

throughout their school careers in order to overcome their learning difficulties, and make an active contribution to society. The severe difficulties in learning which they experience often result from neurological dysfunction or brain damage. The consequent altered processes may affect the rate of learning, but do not result in a general incapacity to learn. Such altered processes result in a delay, in some or all of the main areas of general development, and sensory and physical impairment which are caused either by the direct result of neurological damage or through the way in which those in contact with the child restrict his or her experiences. Children with severe learning difficulties can be identified by marked limitations in learning across all aspects of development, though some may show particular disabilities or relative assets in some areas (DES, 1990). Those who have profound and multiple learning difficulties are functioning at the earliest levels of development (less than one-fifth of their chronological age) and have additional difficulties of vision, hearing or physical functioning (Hogg and Lambe, 1988).

Stephen, for example, is 10 but is at an early stage of development and has physical difficulties. The results of assessment included the following descriptions of his ability:

Sitting Stephen can sit with support.

Rolling He can roll around the classroom. He can also move by pushing with his feet while lying on his back.

Reaching He reaches well with both arms to the same side although he has difficulty crossing his midline. He can reach for things higher than his midline when sitting.

Fine Motor He finds it difficult to open his hands and grasp objects, but after massage his performance improves. He uses a tight palmar grip only.

Personal and Social Education He has a tongue thrust and eating is a lengthy process. He manages to eat mashed food when it is placed in one side of his mouth. He can take a loaded spoon of food to his mouth.

Toileting He remains dry and clean for most of the day but has to be toileted at regular intervals.

English (Language and Communication) Stephen likes people. He has a ready smile and uses his whole body in an enthusiastic welcome routine with familiar adults. He will indicate that he does not want things by turning away or pushing objects from him. He shakes his head for 'no', and uses a nod for yes.

Maths He can select familiar objects from a choice of two. He constantly 'eye points' to two familiar and similar objects in a group of three.

Children with autism display difficulties in social relations and are resistant to changes in routine. Excessive bizarre repetitive behaviours are often displayed. John, like Stephen, is also 10. If left alone he will walk around the room flicking the pages of a telephone directory. He shows indifference to adults and children and avoids eye contact. He does not speak spontaneously but will sometimes 'echo' the last few words spoken to him.

IDENTIFICATION

Until quite recently the identification of special educational needs was concerned primarily with assessing children's intellectual ability relative to that of their peers. Tasks were presented and success defined by criteria which were used to produce a measure of the quality of intellectual development either through an intelligence (IQ) score or a developmental quotient. However, as Hogg and Sebba (1986a) point out, 'global psychometric assessment which produces an overall score as an indicator of general ability may be misleading with a child whose severe sensory or physical impairments depress the total score relative to his or her score in each area of development outside the impaired modality' (p. 2). More recently, criterion-referenced methods of assessment have been used to identify special educational needs. Pupils are 'baselined' by the identification of the skills they possess; programme planning is aimed at teaching immediately above the level at which the child shows competence (see Lacey *et al.*, 1991). Hogg and Sebba (1986b), however, caution that problems may also be experienced with this method of identification of need, as check-lists used to monitor progress can be narrowly defined and the lack of skills attained may reflect the lack of educational opportunities available.

Diagnosis of autism must be based on an informed interpretation of behaviour. Frith (1989) emphasises that an important criterion for diagnosis is concerned with impairments of language and communication: 'Impairments can range from no speech at all to merely delayed language acquisition and odd uses of language, including gesture and body language' (p. 12).

WHY DO SUCH DIFFICULTIES OCCUR?

The causes of severe learning difficulties include prenatal influences, chromosomal abnormalities, disorders of metabolism and trauma at the prenatal or perinatal stages. In many cases it is not difficult to identify the relevant aetiological factors but such information is only useful to a teacher if it helps to identify the educational needs of the child. Down's syndrome, for example, is by far the most common genetic cause of impaired intellectual functioning but the physical signs and disabilities are many and varied and there is no clear relationship between them and mental ability levels; those possessing many of the characteristics are just as likely as those with few to have higher ability levels.

Down's syndrome is the most widely known chromosome abnormality but there are others which can cause severe mental and physical retardation. They include the partial deletion of chromosomes which produces such conditions as 'Cri du chat' and 'Wolf' syndromes, and sex-linked chromosomal abnormalities. Less common than chromosomal defects are simple gene disorders, some of which result in metabolic malfunctions. One such condition, which is now preventable, is Phenylketonuria. Through a simple blood test, which is given after birth to all babies, the condition can be reliably detected and a low phenylalanine diet can be prescribed to prevent the otherwise inevitable progressive damage to the brain. Problems associated with severe difficulties in learning can also occur at the perinatal stage and damage can occur after birth through infections, malnutrition (although this is rare in Britain and is usually associated with abnormal environments or eccentric diets) or as a result of both accidental and non-accidental injury.

Research into the causes of autism is still at an early stage but it is generally believed to stem from organic dysfunctioning. The nature of the dysfunctioning and the reasons for its occurrence remain unknown. Frith (1989) warns against assuming a single cause and suggests a chain of events: hazard, followed by havoc, followed by harm. The 'hazard' may be due to a range of pre, peri and postnatal problems which cause 'havoc' in neural development, and result in harm to the developing brain systems.

However, it is not the aetiology alone which creates severe educational problems for the child; it is the interplay between aetiology and the problems encountered in the physical and social environments which exacerbate their difficulties in learning. Fraser (1984) suggests that the ways in which a child becomes a fully functioning member of society are dependent on *handicapping factors* which include the physical and social environment together with the effects of the impairment. He maintains that children become handicapped through the reduction of those experiences, which would enable them to relate to the organisation of the physical and social world, and to the attitudes that society demonstrates towards them. Such restrictions are of two kinds, both based on an underestimation of a pupil's ability which may result in a mismatch between the learning opportunities required and the educational experiences offered.

The first is concerned with the opportunities given to pupils to make decisions and exercise choices. Mistaken views about their abilities often result in professionals encouraging pupils to become dependent, rather than independent, learners. Through the self-advocacy movement people with severe learning difficulties have started to articulate their distaste for the inhibiting dependency-creating relationships determined by many professionals. The skills needed to gain control over their own lives should underpin the curriculum for all pupils, including those with special educational needs. Self awareness, decision making, choosing and taking on responsibilities are essential competencies which allow pupils to become active participants in society and capable of achieving as much independence as possible. Encouraging pupils to make decisions for themselves can often be extremely demanding for the teacher. Not only is it difficult to ascertain what a pupil wants (as is the case of pupils with communication problems, particularly those with autism or profound and multiple learning difficulties) but it can also challenge the learning opportunities chosen by teachers, based on their implicit values and standards, when pupils make unexpected or even unwelcome choices (Tilstone, 1991).

The second is concerned with the physical environment which is provided for a pupil. Severe difficulties in learning can be minimised if care is taken in devising the physical environment. The built environment can be accessed by providing ramps for wheelchairs and hoists for bathing, and disability can be reduced by using personal aids and appliances. Pupils with profound multiple learning difficulties may be able to use a communication prosthesis, or those with severe learning difficulties may employ a manual signing system (Makaton, for example).

EDUCATIONAL, PERSONAL AND SOCIAL CONSEQUENCES

Historically children with severe learning difficulties have lived a 'life apart', often in institutions in remote rural areas but also in segregated schools, training centres and residential homes. More recently children with severe difficulties in learning have come to be seen as having the same rights as other children; to the services offered through health, education and other community resources. The 1981 Education Act requires that following thorough assessment, a statement of the child's special educational needs should be made which identifies the forms of special help needed. Once identified, consideration should then, and only then, be given to how and where such provision should be made. The practice of segregated special education is slowly being eroded and LEA integration policies for all children with special educational needs have made it possible for many children with severe learning difficulties to be educated in mainstream schools. Special schools will, Fish (1985) reminds us, need to exist as long as there are limitations on what can be provided in mainstream schools, but they should no longer be an automatic choice.

Individual integration projects have rarely been critically evaluated but a high level of interaction between children has been observed (Carpenter *et al.*, 1986; Lewis and Carpenter, 1990) and small-scale studies have shown that children learn socially appropriate behaviours through modelling and that play becomes more normal if integration is commenced early (Mittler and Farrell, 1987). It is, however, accepted that integration is most successful when there is a clear LEA policy; adequate staffing; staff trained to meet the needs of pupils with severe learning difficulties; and suitable resources. It is also clear that a whole school approach is essential to the effectiveness of integration – there are implications for all teachers within the school, not only those directly teaching individual children with special needs. Ainscow and Florek (1989) consider a whole school approach as being a philosophical and practical drive towards true comprehensive education but the Warnock Report outlined a framework for integration with a number of levels within which, for example, integration can signify the absorption of pupils with profound and multiple learning difficulties into classes of children with severe learning difficulties. Another strategy which falls short of full integration but which has been successfully employed in many schools has been the provision of 'links' in which pupils and teachers from a special school join a mainstream school for shared learning and teaching. Apart from the benefits for children with special educational needs there are benefits for mainstream pupils; documented accounts show positive changes in the attitudes of mainstream pupils towards their special school peers (Carpenter *et al.*, 1991; Quicke *et al.*, 1990). These innovations can contribute to the elimination of one of Fraser's (1984) handicapping factors: the negative attitudes of society.

Some pupils with severe learning difficulties exhibit behaviours commonly referred to as *challenging*. Zarkowska and Clements (1988) estimate that between 50 and 60 per cent of people with severe learning difficulties present significant behaviour problems; tantrums and aggression may be exhibited by all children but self-mutilation and bizarre, violent, repetitious, ritualistic and non-compliant behaviours tend to be more prevalent in children with severe learning difficulties (see also Presland, 1989). Teachers need the skills to deal with these behaviours, to eliminate them and to provide the child with more appropriate modes of conduct. Intervention in the past has relied on behavioural techniques which modify the behaviour and build up new skills (Yule and Carr, 1980; Foxen and McBrien, 1981; McBrien and Foxen, 1981) but more attention has recently been given to the building of relationships through non-aversive strategies which encourage communication and social interaction (McGee *et al.*, 1987; La Vigna and Donnellan, 1986).

SPECIAL SKILLS AND RESOURCES

It is self evident that pupils with severe learning difficulties need 'good' teachers. The debate on what constitutes good practice is well documented and Smith (1988) identified a good teacher, from his perspective as a headteacher, as someone who:

1 always recognises and minimises tensions;
2 makes children feel good about themselves, recognising that they are individuals and need individual attention;
3 believes strongly in a work ethos and on-task behaviour, but does so without negative pressures;
4 views children and parents in a positive way and understands the importance of working partnerships;
5 avoids shouting and bullying and is a quiet, firm disciplinarian who sees positive control as a means of stimulating learning;
6 gives praise rather than criticism;
7 recognises and uses a child's enthusiasms and talents;
8 sees a wide-ranging curriculum as the most effective way to encourage basic skills;
9 sees creativity and curiosity as the key to learning experiences;
10 sees change as positive and necessary in any progressive institution; and
11 varies teaching styles to suit individual children.

Underpinning Smith's inventory is the need for detailed and objective observation and recording, both of which are essential elements in the accurate identification of the changes of behaviour which pupils exhibit in response to teaching. Some of these changes will be extremely small, particularly when physical and sensory impairments obstruct learning. The ability to observe and record accurately is a skill which is often taken for granted and frequently undervalued. It needs to be carried out systematically and rigorously if a teacher is to ascertain not only *what* learning has occurred but also *how* that learning has taken place. All pupils do not learn in the same way, and it is essential to know how each child responds to stimuli in order to decide on the appropriate teaching style necessary to encourage curiosity and creativity. Detailed observation and recording of the learning process also enable teachers to examine and re-examine the learning experiences offered to their pupils. Consequently a continual enquiry into the decisions which govern the selection of the curriculum content is encouraged. It is often difficult for teachers to determine priorities within a curriculum which is designed to allow pupils to make an active contribution to society. The slow rate of progress of some of the pupils may lead to the constant repetition of learning experiences, the result of which is pupil boredom and frustration. Teachers need to evaluate their work constantly both in terms of curriculum content and their own personal ideals if they are to arrive at a curriculum which addresses individual needs. Teaching is a fluid and complex activity which requires analysis, reflection, change, precise observation and the recording of what pupils are actually doing in a variety of situations.

The skills of detailed observation depend primarily on an in-depth knowledge of early stages of child development. Many children are functioning within Piaget's sensori-motor period. An understanding therefore of the stages from birth, when the child is virtually a reflex organism, through to the development of language and the ability to symbolise the world, is essential if a teacher is to formulate a curriculum matching a child's abilities and needs. Assessment will depend upon a clear understanding of the ways in which children develop; intervention will involve the teaching of skills which normal children acquire naturally. For example, it is often necessary to teach pupils to look, to reach out for objects, to explore their environment or to interact with adults or peers and to indicate what they want.

Such teaching cannot be undertaken alone. It requires collaboration and a team approach. The team involved with a pupil within the classroom may consist of a teacher and a special support assistant, but it is likely to include other professionals too. It is not unusual for one pupil to have contact with physio-, speech and occupational therapists together with a psychologist and members of the sensory impairment team. Ouvry (1987) regards all members of a multi-disciplinary team as 'developmental therapists' with particular areas of expertise, who contribute to the physical, mental, social and emotional progress of the child. However, multi-disciplinary involvement needs co-ordination and teachers need the skills to resolve conflict, to remove professional barriers, to promote effective communication and to create an organisational structure which will enable all members of the team to contribute to a shared goal – that of encouraging growth in all areas of development.

Teamwork also involves working collaboratively with parents. 'Parents as partners' is a slogan which has been adopted by all sectors of education, but the crucial importance of a dialogue between parents and children must be fully recognised in work with children with severe learning difficulties if the essential information which they possess about their child is to be made available to, and fully utilised by, all members of the multi-disciplinary team (Mittler and Mittler, 1982). Evidence is available on the effectiveness of parents as teachers of pupils with severe learning difficulties (Cameron, 1986; McConachie, 1986; Russell, 1991), but 'parents as partners' has wider possibilities. It can involve an interactive process of teachers working *through* parents; learning from them; learning with them; learning about them and at the same time respecting and recognising their particular needs. Partnership rests on the recognition of the uniqueness of each family and the parents' wish to be involved at various stages and at different levels throughout their child's education. Hornby (1989) offers a useful model of parental participation which highlights the professional expertise necessary to sustain 'true partnership'.

Teaching children with severe learning difficulties continues to be a challenge. Fundamental changes have taken place in curriculum design, content and delivery, influenced at one level by social, political and economic factors, also at another by recent research. The aims of the curriculum are the same for all children and should reflect personal autonomy and independence. In the early 1980s the traditional model of curriculum design reflected a step by step approach to the teaching of skills through precisely defined objectives and task analysis (see, for example, Crawford, 1980; Gardner *et al.*, 1983). More recently teachers have been experimenting with a broader curriculum framework which allows greater emphasis to be placed on partnership and the development of co-operative and study skills, problem solving, and individual responsibility for learning. The interactive approach (Smith, 1988; McConkey, 1988) is designed to encourage such wide-ranging and meaningful partnerships and allows teachers to select and structure the environment in order to facilitate and maximise cognitive processes. Communication and collaboration are central to this process-oriented approach which extends beyond the acquisition of skills taught in isolation. In order to re-evaluate practices teachers need to be aware of recent developments through adequate in-service training, but Robson *et al.* (1988) argue that working with people with disabilities is devalued by society and as a result in-service training has not kept pace with the changing needs of pupils, nor the emerging patterns of service delivery. 'It is not only a matter of the numbers of staff that can take advantage of training opportunities, but also of information and knowledge which are already available reaching only a small minority of staff working in the service' (p. 3). Unfortunately many teachers are therefore unaware of new developments, which could radically influence their practice.

CONCLUSION

At a time of rapid changes in education, it is essential for all teachers to be aware of current research and national developments. The Education Reform Act of 1988 has proved a mixed blessing. All pupils are now entitled to receive a broad and balanced curriculum, a development welcomed by teachers of pupils with severe learning difficulties, many of whom had been dissatisfied with a previously limited curriculum with an over-emphasis on skills. Early curriculum documents, however, failed to mention these pupils. The dangers of a situation in which there were two distinct groups of children (one inside, the other outside the National Curriculum) became apparent. Teachers were forced, frequently with little help from their Local Education Authorities, to consider the wider implications, to adapt specific requirements and to seek help from colleagues, often outside their own local authority. Teachers have responded with energy and enthusiasm and subsequent publications based on the assessment of good practice are readily available. The works of Aherne *et al.* (1990a; 1990b), Fagg *et al.* (1990a; 1990b) and Ackerman and Mount (1991) are particularly useful as they discuss the implications of the core subjects for the full range of children with severe learning difficulties. These authors emphasise the possibilities of a shared curriculum and easier access to mainstream activities through the adoption of a common framework and common terminology.

It has become evident that most of the programmes of study in the core areas are already in use in the curricula of many schools and useful evidence of good practice has been identified by a team based at Cambridge Institute of Education led by Judy Sebba and funded by the National Curriculum Council. Their publication *Curriculum Guidance* will be welcomed in all schools.

A report on a series of visits made by HMI in 1989–90 to twenty-six ordinary and fifty special schools catering for the whole range of

SEN, including severe learning difficulties, revealed 'a widespread commitment by teachers to planning for maximum possible access to the National Curriculum for all children' (p. 9) but the report emphasises the continuing need to review and develop the curriculum if access to the National Curriculum is to be fully realised. A rigorous review of existing practice, encouraged by the National Curriculum Council's (1990) document *Guidance Three: The Whole Curriculum*, has enabled teachers to reconsider the learning needs of individual pupils, to re-examine their priorities and methodology, and to extend the curriculum on offer (Ouvry, 1991). However, despite its advantages, teachers of pupils with severe learning difficulties have reservations about some aspects of the National Curriculum; they are: concerns over tokenism, the nature of standardised assessment, and the rigid linking of key stages and programmes of study to the ages of pupils.

In an effort to ensure access for all pupils, teachers are aware that there should be no distortion of the programmes of study or the attainment targets to a degree which makes activities meaningless or which fails to reflect the need of individuals. The overwhelming amount of documentation issued to schools by the Department of Education and Science, the National Curriculum Council (NCC) and the Schools Examinations and Assessment Council (SEAC) has made it difficult to keep the National Curriculum in perspective. It must be a part of every school's whole curriculum and the priorities determined by the needs of individual pupils will need to include elements not usually found in the curricula of mainstream schools.

The National Curriculum has encouraged many schools to consider a whole school approach to assessment. The need to address the particular problems of Records of Achievement has made teachers re-think the monitoring of pupils' learning, including the pupils' own contribution to the process, and re-evaluate classroom practices and processes. However it is assessment by means of Standard Assessment Tasks (SATs) which has given most rise for concern; experience so far has revealed that testing material and assessment procedures are not always relevant to the needs of pupils with severe learning difficulties. A continuing question is whether SATs are necessary for pupils with severe learning difficulties and what might replace them? SEAC has been surprisingly silent on the subject of assessment and pupils with severe learning difficulties despite constant enquiries from the field.

Rouse, in a perceptive critique of the uncertainty and confusion surrounding the assessment debate, emphasises:

> We must not be allowed to be overwhelmed by systems designed to compare schools and which are only capable of saying that some of our students are still working at Level 1. It is essential to preserve and nurture those forms of assessment which will enhance our professionalism, improve the quality of teaching and learning, and celebrate the achievements of our children across the whole of their development.
>
> (Rouse, 1991, p. 309)

REFERENCES

Ackerman, D. and Mount, H. (1991) *Literacy for All*, London: David Fulton.

Aherne, P., Thornber, A., Fagg, S. and Skelton, S. (1990a) *Communication for All*, London: David Fulton.

——(1990b) *Mathematics for All*, London: David Fulton.

Ainscow, M. and Florek, A. (1989) *Special Educational Needs: Towards a Whole School Approach*, London: David Fulton.

Cameron, R.J. (ed.) (1986) *Portage: Pre-schoolers, Parents and Professionals. Ten Years of Achievement in the U.K.*, Windsor: NFER/Nelson.

Carpenter, B., Lewis, A. and Moore, J. (1986) 'Integration: a project involving children with severe learning difficulties and first school children', *Mental Handicap*, 14, 4, 152–7.

Carpenter, B., Lindoe, S. and Moore, J. (1991) 'Changing attitudes', in C. Tilstone (ed.) *Teaching Pupils with Severe Learning Difficulties: Practical Approaches*, London: David Fulton.

Crawford, N.B. (ed.) (1980) *Curriculum Planning for the ESN(s) Child*, Kidderminster: BIMH.

Department of Education and Science (1978) *Special Educational Needs: Report of the Committee of Enquiry into the Education of Handicapped Children and Young People*, London: HMSO.

——(1990) *Staffing for Pupils with Special Educational Needs. Circular No.11/90*, London: DES.

Fagg, S., Aherne, P., Skelton, S. and Thornber, A. (1990a) *Entitlement for All in Practice*, London: David Fulton.

——(1990b) *Science for All*, London: David Fulton.

Fish, J. (1985) *Special Education: The Way Ahead*, Milton Keynes: Open University Press.

Foxen, T. and McBrien, J. (1981) *Trainees Workbook. Education of the Developmentally Young*, Manchester: Manchester University Press.

Fraser, B. (1984) *Society, Schools and Handicap*, Stratford: NCSE.

Frith, U. (1989) *Autism: Explaining the Enigma*, Oxford: Basil Blackwell.

Gardner, J., Murphy, J. and Crawford, N. (1983) *The Skills Analysis Model*, Kidderminster: BIMH.

Hogg, J. and Lambe, S. (1988) *Children and Adults with Profound Retardation and Multiple Handicaps Attending School or Social Education Centre: A Final Report On The Needs Of Their Families, Foster Parents And Relatives*, London: Mencap.

Hogg, J. and Sebba, J. (1986a) *Profound Retardation and Multiple Impairment Volume 1. Development and Learning*, London: Croom Helm.

——(1986b) *Profound Retardation and Multiple Impairment Volume 2. Education and Therapy*, London: Croom Helm.

Hornby, G. (1989) 'A model for parent participation', *British Journal of Special Education*, 4, 161–2.

Lacey, P., Smith, B. and Tilstone, C. (1991) 'Influences on curriculum design, and on assessment', in C. Tilstone (ed.) *Teaching Pupils with Severe Learning Difficulties: Practical Approaches*, London: David Fulton.

La Vigna, G.W. and Donnellan, A.M. (1986) *Alternatives to Punishment: Solving Behaviour Problems with Non-Aversive Strategies*, New York: Irvington Publications.

Lewis, A. and Carpenter, B. (1990) 'Discourse in an integrated school setting, between six and seven year old non-handicapped children and peers with severe learning difficulties', in W.I. Frazer (ed.) *Key Issues in Mental Retardation*, London: Routledge.

McBrien, J. and Foxen, T. (1981) *Instructors Handbook. Education of the Developmentally Young*, Manchester: Manchester University Press.

McConachie, H. (1986) *Parents and Young Mentally Handicapped Children. A Review of Research Issues*, London: Croom Helm.

McConkey, R. (1988) 'Interaction: the name of the game', in B. Smith (ed.) *Interactive Approaches to the Education of Children with Severe Learning Difficulties,* Birmingham: Westhill College.

McGee, J., Menolascino, F., Hobbs, D. and Menousek, P. (1987) *Gentle Teaching*, New York: Human Sciences Press Inc.

Mittler, P. and Farrell, P. (1987) 'Can children with severe learning difficulties be educated in ordinary schools?', *European Journal of Special Education*, 2, 221–36.

Mittler, P. and Mittler, H. (1982) *Partnership with Parents*, Stratford: National Council for Special Education.

National Curriculum Council (1990) *Curriculum Guidance Three: The Whole Curriculum*, York: The National Curriculum Council.

Ouvry, C. (1987) *Educating Children with Profound Handicaps*, Kidderminster: BIMH.

——(1991) 'Access for pupils with profound and multiple learning difficulties', in R. Ashdown, B. Carpenter and K. Bovair (eds) *The Curriculum Challenge*, Lewes: Falmer Press.

Presland, J.L. (1989) *Overcoming Difficult Behaviour*, Kidderminster: BIMH.

Quicke, J., Beasley, K. and Morrison, C. (1990) *Challenging Prejudice through Education. The Story of a Mental Handicap Awareness Curriculum Project*, London: Falmer Press.

Robson, C., Sebba, J., Mittler, P. and Davies, G. (1988) *In-Service Training and Special Educational Needs. Running Short School-Focussed Courses*, Manchester: Manchester University Press.

Rouse, M. (1991) 'Assessment, the National Curriculum and special educational needs: confusion or consensus?', in R. Ashdown, B. Carpenter and K. Bovair (eds) *The Curriculum Challenge*, London: Falmer Press.

Russell, P. (1991) 'Access to the National Curriculum for parents', in R. Ashdown, B. Carpenter and K. Bovair (eds) *The Curriculum Challenge*, London: Falmer Press.

Smith, B. (1988) *Interactive Approaches to the Education of Children with Severe Learning Difficulties*, Birmingham: Westhill College.

Smith, R. (1988) 'What makes a good teacher?', *Child Education,* 10–11.

Tilstone, C. (1991) 'Pupils' views', in C. Tilstone (ed.) *Teaching Pupils with Severe Learning Difficulties: Practical Approaches*, London: David Fulton.

Yule, W. and Carr, J. (1980) *Behaviour Modification for People with Mental Handicaps* (Second Edition), London: Croom Helm.

Zarkowska, E. and Clements, J. (1988) *Problem Behaviour in People with Severe Learning Difficulties*, London: Croom Helm.

5

SPEECH AND LANGUAGE DIFFICULTIES

Carol Miller

All teachers will have encountered at some time a pupil who has some kind of difficulty in speech and/or language – maybe one who is seen regularly for speech therapy or one who has been considered for placement in a special class for children with speech and language disorders. Their difficulties are varied. The following are examples of children aged between 4 and 5 years with different kinds of speech and language difficulty:

Ann is a very quiet child who rarely attempts to enter into conversation. She is able to select objects correctly when asked and appropriately mimes activities such as drinking, eating and writing. When asked to name a ball; a spoon; a car; a brush, she says 'ba' for each of them.

Martin is a lively child who understands conversation appropriately for his age and talks a great deal but is apparently unaware that others find him very difficult to understand. Examples of his single words are: 'eepi' for sleeping; 'rididi' for Christmas tree; 'wade' for flower; 'pee' for three and 'oyi' for horse.

David is a sociable child who is well aware of his difficulties in speaking and uses a great deal of gesture to communicate. Examples of his connected speech include:

'knife for tut dem' (a knife to cut them)
'e yoti in e water e we tow' (the horse is in the water and the cow)
'me no hnow' (I don't know)

These children would immediately concern a teacher, but children with speech and language difficulties show a wide range of characteristics, some of which are not so immediately evident to an observer. The group includes children who talk very little, those whose speech is difficult to understand and those who do not understand what others say to them. As the children get older, difficulties may also be noted in the written forms of language. In particular, in the infant classroom, it is important to be aware that the child who never seems to listen, the child who is very quiet or the child who always has a cold may have a difficulty in learning to talk and to understand others.

Since spoken language shows considerable variation across individuals, it is important to be clear about the difference between a normal variation in development and a genuine problem. Accents and dialects are not speech disorders nor is the speech of a child who is developing bilingually; these are part of the wide variety of patterns of spoken language. Crystal (1988) suggests that 'language becomes a matter for concern when it impedes rather than facilitates communication. When it draws too much attention to itself, the listener or reader is distracted from the meaning which the speaker or writer is attempting to convey' (p. 9). The development of language in children also shows great variation and consideration must necessarily be given to the child's age and stage of development in determining whether or not a child has a problem. Lahey (1988) defines a speech disorder as 'any disruption in the learning or use of one's native language as evidenced by language behaviours that are different from (but not superior to) those expected given a child's chronological age' (p. 21).

In considering language disability, it is important to keep normal language development in mind as this will help in the identification and analysis of language difficulty. Successful language results from the integration of its content, its form and its use, so that in the normal pattern of development, these components interact with each other as the effectiveness of the child's communicative skills increases (Bloom and Lahey, 1978).

Content refers to the ideas and messages that are encoded by language. The child's development of content depends on the interaction between knowledge and context so that understanding develops from real situations with activities and interactions with other people. The child begins to associate events which are similar and remembers them for future reference. The content of language concerns knowledge of objects, relationships between objects and relationships between events. Linguists describe this as the semantic level of language, that is, the level of language concerned with meaning.

Form refers to the set of sounds and words and the rules for combining them. In spoken language, it is the method for combining sound with meaning. Signing would be another form, as would written language. When discussing these aspects of language, linguists talk of phonology or the sound system of a language, morphology, the small units which make up words and syntax or the combining of words in utterances.

Use is concerned with the functions of language and the contexts in which it is used. It relates to the reasons why people speak and the choices they make in speaking. This area of language is known as pragmatics.

Problems of language can occur in any aspects of its content, its form or its use, or in any combination of these. Children showing problems of language form may have difficulties with the system of sounds of the language or with the meaning-carrying parts of words, the morphemes. They may have problems with words or phrases. For example, a 4-year-old boy, talking about the treats available when he went with his father to football matches said:

'me o de hwee me o de dwing'.

Directly translated, this was:

'me don't get sweets me only get drinks'.

The adult who knew the child well knew that he meant:

'I don't get sweets I only get drinks'.

The main obstacle to understanding this child's speech lay in his use of sounds. For example, 'd' replaces 'g' in 'get' and 'hw' is substituted for 'sw' in 'sweets'. 'dr' at the beginning of 'drinks' is replaced by 'dw' and the final 's' signifying a plural, is omitted. The word 'only' lacks its final syllable. There are also grammatical differences between this and adult speech: 'me' is used instead of 'I'.

The child with a problem of language content has difficulties in conceptual development and in the ideas that are necessary to make up language. This difficulty is frequently linked with poor cognitive skills but may also indicate other problems. In the example below, a child, age 7 years 2 months, was unable to sort categories of words such as animals, transport and food. The following is an extract from a conversation with him (T = teacher, C = child):

T   What's a dog?
C   Cat. It's only a dog.
T   Is it a fruit or an animal?
C   Animal
T   What's a cat?
C   A fruit

(Stackhouse and Miller, 1990)

Children with difficulties in language use might talk about something out of context or may *ramble* in an irrelevant manner, regardless of the conversational partner. The example above illustrates how a problem of content results in a problem of use and a breakdown in communication between adult and child. Some children with these difficulties may appear to be very articulate but will sometimes say bizarre things. They may address the teacher inappropriately and sometimes fail to use pronouns such as 'you' or 'me' correctly. It may sometimes appear that they are not taking sufficient account of their conversational partner and sometimes they fail to make satisfactory relationships with other children because of their language inadequacy.

However, problems of language rarely fall neatly into these categories. Because of the close interdependence of the levels of language, one aspect will usually affect another. So, for example, children with problems of content will frequently show anomalies of form since conceptual development is necessary in order to learn about the structure of language. Problems of content may also affect use since the child who does not easily associate ideas may speak inappropriately for the situation.

Exact figures for the number of children with speech and language difficulties are not easy to find. Definitions vary and the populations studied show a range of characteristics. However, a review of surveys suggests that there is a high occurrence of speech problems in early infancy and that around 5 per cent of children entering school are unable to make themselves understood (Webster and McConnell, 1987). There is, however, no reason to believe that all of these children will have special educational needs. Delayed speech and language is probably the most common form of speech and language difficulty in children and while some children will require the intervention of an experienced teacher or a speech and language therapist, together with advice and support to the parents, many of them will develop adequate understanding and expression of language with no specific help. What is most important is that parents and teachers should observe the progress of the child's communication skills since the particular nature of this development might give indications of later difficulties. In particular, the time that a child begins to talk, together with the rate of development of a child's speech and language, are relevant. The language of the majority of children develops at the expected time and at a rate comparable with most other children. A few children start early and develop rapidly; others may start late and then catch up with their peers. The children who are of most concern start late and do not catch up because the rate of development is excessively slow, patchy, stops or regresses. These children may require continuing specialist help and have often been described as having a language disorder rather than a delay since their language development does not resemble the usual pattern but deviates from it. The need to note carefully the course of speech and language development carries with it the implication that those working with young children should have well-developed observation skills based on adequate knowledge and experience in this area of child development. Nursery and infant teachers play an important part in the identification of children's speech and language problems. They have experience which enables them to compare the development of children and their day-to-day contact with children means that they can collect examples of what a child can say and appears to understand. Careful observation will show whether a child follows simple verbal directions or whether a gesture is always needed for the child to 'come here' or 'go and get the . . .'. While many children still have unclear speech when they start school, the child whose speech remains unintelligible may be in need of some help.

A broad categorisation of problems of communication divides them into those affecting speech, language, voice and fluency. The first two will mainly be the concern of this chapter and will be addressed later but voice and fluency require some mention. Problems of fluency, in which the features of stress, rhythm and intonation can be disrupted, may be related, in some cases, to disorders of language. Early disfluency should not be ignored since it may be associated with a language difficulty. Advanced disfluency, manifested as the full-blown adult stutter or stammer (the terms are synonymous), may lead to wider problems if the individual avoids speaking in certain situations or if fear of stuttering leads them to change words. Problems of voice, in which the voice is persistently hoarse or even absent, may be related to physiological and/or psychological causes. If ignored, these too may lead to, or arise from, problems in social interaction. For further discussions of disfluency and voice disorders readers can refer to Dalton and Hardcastle (1989) and to Wilson (1987).

Classifications of speech and language disorders have fallen traditionally into two general categories: one which gives a name to a problem and one which indicates a cause or underlying problem. Typical of the first approach is the way in which many of the terms used to name speech and language problems have the medical prefix 'dys', indicating a lack of function or ability. We thus find the terms, dysphasia, dyspraxia, dysarthria and dyslexia referring to various forms of spoken and written language difficulty. One of the problems associated with such a classification is that terms are interpreted in various ways by different people and the fact that each term covers a wide range of signs and symptoms and gives little indication of the needs of the affected person. The second type of classification indicates what is assumed to be the main contributor to the problem, so that we find, for example, categories such as hearing impairment, cleft palate, mental handicap. A similar criticism to that made of the first approach can be made of this classification in that it gives little indication of the nature of the speech and/or language difficulty involved and, since the individual's ability to communicate will vary in every case, it provides us with no assistance in deciding what the person needs.

More recent models of speech and language disorder have focused on descriptions, either of the language of the individual or of the strengths and weaknesses underlying their communicative ability. Bloom and Lahey's (1978) division of language into content, form and use, described above, is helpful here, as it gives an indication of the area of language we are dealing with. Obviously, more details are required if programmes of teaching and therapy are to be designed and various methods of analysis of the speech and language are therefore employed. Such analyses might describe the grammar of a sample of language, or the specific sounds used or the nature of the interaction between a child and others. By comparing these analyses with data on normal language, indications are gained on where to focus the programme of remediation. The description of strengths and weaknesses relies on observations of the language processing abilities of the individual so that information is gathered on where and how these are breaking down. For example, while two children may show similar patterns in their speech-sound production, one may have difficulty discriminating between speech sounds made by other people, yet have no hearing loss, and the other may have difficulty in coordinating the parts of the mouth required to make the speech sounds. Such distinctions are critical to the design of effective remediation work.

CAUSES AND INFLUENCES

Research into the factors which influence the occurrence of speech and language disorders has focused on sensory, physical, neurological, cognitive, genetic and environmental factors. A summary is provided here, and the reader is referred to Byers-Brown and Edwards (1989) for a more comprehensive review.

Family history

There is some evidence that some speech and language problems run in families. In certain cases investigations have revealed that more than one member of a family is affected, either within the same generation or across generations. In addition, there is evidence that males are affected more frequently than females. From these studies it has been concluded that there is a possible genetic factor in some language disorders, but the specific nature of this has not yet been identified.

Neurological explanations

There are suggestions that some children may have abnormalities in the developing nervous system and that some may have a particular delay in those areas of the brain responsible for language. Where it is known that a child has suffered brain injury or disease, then the particular site and timing of the damage may cause a child to be at risk for language disorder, either developmental or acquired.

Perinatal factors

To date, no specific occurrence around the time of birth has been associated with language disorder but the observation has been made that the more perinatal complications that exist, together with adverse environmental factors, the more risk there is that a child will show problems in the development of language.

Hearing loss

Profound hearing loss, acquired prenatally or early in childhood, can have severe implications for the development of speech and language. Additionally, there are suggestions that repeated middle ear infections (otitis media) in childhood are associated with language disorder. However, there are also observations that when the ear infections are successfully treated, medically or surgically, then, provided the child has no other serious problems, language development usually proceeds normally. Bishop and Edmundson (1986) conclude that 'while otitis media alone may not be a crucial determinant of speech and language difficulties, it may interact with other risk factors, so that it becomes important if the child is already vulnerable because of a hazardous perinatal history' (p. 335). (See also Chapter 8 for more information on this.)

Cognitive impairment

There are differing views on the relationship between language and thinking. In the research on language disorders, a chicken and egg situation is apparent, that is, where a child shows both language and cognitive difficulties, it is not easy to determine which has come first. However, many children with low cognitive functioning show disruption in language skills.

Environmental factors

There are observations that many children with language disabilities come from disadvantaged backgrounds. However, it should also be noted that many of these children are born at biological risk. For example, they may be of very low birth weight or be born to mothers who are in poor health or living in inadequate conditions.

It is likely that environmental factors interact with other conditions to give particular developmental problems such as language disorders.

A conclusion to this brief summary might be that so far, a single, specific cause for language disorder has not been found and indeed, Bishop (1987) has suggested that 'we should give serious consideration to the possibility that aetiological factors may interact in the causation of developmental language disorders, so that the effect of several factors together is greater than the sum of individual effects' (p. 6).

ASSOCIATED CONSEQUENCES OF SPEECH AND LANGUAGE DIFFICULTIES

The effects of speech and language difficulty will vary according to its specific nature in the individual child. A full description of each child's language and its underlying skills is essential if we are to identify the particular help that a child will need from teachers and others. There is some evidence that children with speech and language difficulties are less mature than their peers. There are also reports of aggressive behaviour, withdrawal, social inadequacy and hyperactivity and one can speculate indefinitely about the genesis and influence of these behaviours. Experienced professionals will confirm that, as with any group, individual differences are the norm. Children with apparently similar levels of language will show very different patterns of communication and it is important to be aware of immense variations in expressive and responsive behaviours when considering the child as a whole. A girl or boy with a serious problem of intelligibility may talk a great deal, providing a challenge to others to maintain communication with the child. Another may be reluctant to talk, yet be appropriately responsive to others.

Several studies have concluded that children with language difficulties have a different experience of communication with adults than those with normally developing speech and language. Stevenson *et al.* (1985) suggest that problems of language structure may give rise to problems in interpersonal relationships while Davis *et al.* (1988) found that in free play, mothers of children with language delay talked less to their children and used more commands than those where there was no delay. It is difficult to know whether the child's language delay is the result of reduced input of language or the reverse but Davis and his colleagues suggest that the mothers may construe or perceive their children differently. They therefore make a case for always seeing a child's difficulty in the context of the whole family. In another study, Conti-Ramsden (1987) concludes that it is not surprising that mothers are less responsive to their language-impaired children in that the children themselves do not request as much from them as younger, normal siblings. While much of the research has focused on relationships between mothers and children, there is no reason to believe that other adults, including fathers, teachers and therapists, will not also react differently to children with language difficulty.

While language skills are inextricably linked and influence each other, comprehension and production of language must also be considered separately. Some children have difficulties understanding the language that they hear whereas others have problems with expression. The National Curriculum in the UK requires children to participate as speakers and listeners in a variety of school activities. For children with speech and language difficulties, speaking and listening may represent very different levels of ability and will need to be given separate consideration in curriculum delivery and in assessment.

While a child's sound system and grammatical structure are mainly complete by the early school years, vocabulary, subtleties of language use and some complex language structures continue to develop throughout childhood. The child with language difficulty may experience problems in some of the day-to-day school experiences which rely on understanding and use of language. The child may have problems in processing specific aspects of language and, depending on the particular nature of the difficulty, this may be seen as poor memory for spoken information, difficulty remembering things in correct order or in understanding fine nuances of language such as are found in jokes, sarcasm or metaphor. There may be difficulties with temporal language and some of the children will be unable to 'play' with language in the way that others make up rhymes and rhythmic chants.

The fine processing skills on which speech and language are founded also relate to the child's ability to develop literacy skills. Reading and spelling difficulties occur frequently when a child has serious speech and language impairment. In particular, there may be problems associating written letters with their sound-values with consequent difficulties in tackling unfamiliar material phonically. A full analysis of a child's reading and spelling error-types may reveal particular patterns of processing in this area of language. For further information on the reading and spelling problems of children with speech and language problems see Stackhouse (1989).

SPECIALIST SKILLS AND RESOURCES

A number of professionals contribute to the care of children with speech and language difficulties, their involvement varying through assessment and ongoing management. The majority of children will have been identified in the pre-school stage, probably as cases of delayed speech and language; however, at school age, teachers may contribute to the identification of children with difficulties through their own observations and the use of screening procedures. Examples of these are the checklists developed by the Association For All Speech Impaired Children (AFASIC, 1991). These provide teachers with procedures which enable them to screen children of 4–5 years and between 6 and 10 years for speech and language difficulties. No special training, equipment or resources are required.

As the relationship between the onset and rate of their speech and language development becomes clearer, the special educational needs of the child may become more apparent. At school entry, the speech and language therapist will, in many cases, already have had contact with the child and its family for a year or more. There will then be an increasing need for cooperative activity between the teacher and the therapist. In addition, the child will probably have been seen by the family doctor and a health visitor for general medical and developmental checks and should have been seen by an audiologist for a full assessment of hearing. Where these professionals are employed in the health service, conscious efforts are required to ensure effective communication between health and educational services although the speech and language therapist may, in fact, be the main 'live' contact between the school and the health service. If the child has a statement of special educational need which identifies speech and language therapy, then it is the responsibility of the Local Education Authority to ensure that this is arranged.

There are various models of service delivery in speech and language therapy and some of these will depend on local arrangements and the availability of therapists. Speech and language therapists are trained to identify and diagnose disorders of communication and to design management programmes. In the case of young children, this will frequently mean discussing and planning with a child's parents and teacher effective ways of encouraging the development of speech and language on a day-to-day basis in the home and the school. There may also be specific activities to be carried out with the child or with groups of children, by the therapist or the teacher or by another professional such as the classroom assistant or the speech and language therapy assistant. A specially qualified support teacher for children with speech and language difficulties may also be available to contribute to the work, in particular advising on the relationship between the speech and language problem and the curriculum. Such advice might include always using short simple sentences when talking to the child or making sure that the child is paired with a suitable partner or group of children in order to participate maximally in classroom activities.

Appraisal of a child's speech and language continues as long as there is contact with the child. Information will be added as the child gives evidence of strengths and weaknesses in differing day-to-day situations and parents and teachers contribute their observations to build up a comprehensive picture of the child's communication. Specific resources available to teachers and parents for this assessment include materials such as *The Pragmatics Profile of Early Communication Skills* (Dewart and Summers, 1988), and *The Primary Language Record* (Barrs *et al.*, 1988). The first of these provides an interview schedule in which the parents or someone who knows the child well describes the child's ability to communicate in various situations. *The Primary Language Record* provides a framework for the assessment and planning of language activities and endorses the roles of pupils, parents and teachers in the learning process. Other publications to help teachers with the assessment and recording of children's communication are increasingly becoming available as materials are developed to support the National Curriculum. The National Oracy Project, for example, has produced valuable ideas which can be used to gain a picture of a child's communication skills (National Oracy Project/ National Curriculum Council, 1991). The speech and language therapist may also use a range of profiling and test procedures which examine specific aspects of the child's language in a variety of contexts. The teacher should always expect full explanations of these and discussion of the likely implications for the child in school.

Assessment of the child's language skills should provide indications for both the specific management of the language difficulties and for any means by which language needs to be modified if the child is to gain access to a broad and balanced curriculum in school. The cross-curricular significance of language is that normally it is the medium for conveying and for assessing knowledge. If the child with a language disorder is not to be disadvantaged, then care will be needed to ensure that the child understands instructions and is able to communicate in some form. Teachers may need to become familiar with alternative and augmentative systems of communication if a particular child uses a non-speech system such as a sign language, a symbol system or a technological communication aid.

All school subjects carry their own vocabulary and special terms which are inextricably linked with the learning of the subject matter; for the child with a language problem, these specialist words and phrases may impede their learning of the subject. Teachers will need to be aware, for example, of the potential difficulties in language involved in a maths or a science lesson and to ensure that any problems in understanding are clarified for every child in a group. One teacher in Oxfordshire, by careful observation of a boy with a language disorder, in mainstream science lessons, was able to identify particular strategies to help him. She noted that: the boy responded much better to questions and instructions when he was named personally in contrast to when he was not named; short simple sentences addressed to him helped his comprehension; he could work successfully if helped by a partner with good reading skills and if he was allowed to record his results in a way which did not depend on writing (Armstrong *et al.*, 1991). 'Differentiation' of the curriculum in ways such as this means that the rights of every child to that curriculum will be observed. For further writing by two experienced teachers about teaching children with language disorders see Hutt (1986) and Donlan and Hutt (1991).

The educational management of children with language disabilities will vary across a range of factors. The majority of children will attend their local mainstream school where they may receive specific help from a speech and language therapist, an educational psychologist, a specialist advisory teacher or the school's special needs coordinator. According to local policy and availability, some children will attend a language unit or special class for a small number of children, attached to a mainstream school. In such a class, children will receive special teaching and therapy according to their particular language needs and will frequently join with the children from the main part of the school wherever their abilities allow. The other main type of educational provision for children with severe communication disorders is a special school which generally takes children either on a residential or a daily basis. In these schools, the whole curriculum and classroom management can take account of the needs of children with speech and language disorders.

The child with a speech and language impairment provides a particular challenge for the teacher, whether in a mainstream classroom or in special provision. The class teacher will be the key person in daily contact with the child in school. Through skilled management of individual and group activity, the child with a speech or language difficulty can be helped to make the most of their education. Recent developments in the school curriculum lay specific emphasis on language skills so that detailed knowledge of language is valuable for all teachers; communication is now an explicit part of every curriculum area. Where there are children with particular language needs, teachers must be able to describe these and discuss with colleagues how they can be met in the classroom. Teachers therefore need a 'language to talk about language'. They need to be clear about the particular language skills required of children in any activity and they need to be aware of the central importance of their own language skills in communicating effectively with children at varying levels of ability. In a recent survey of teachers working with children with speech and language disorders, teachers additionally expressed the need to know how to manage the children in the classroom and how to talk about speech and language impairment with parents and with other professionals (Miller, 1991). These needs are not normally addressed in initial teacher training and the detail required is unlikely to be adequately covered in short courses or in the training courses for other types of special educational needs. In the UK, no special priority has been given to this area of need and there is no mandatory training requirement for teachers but specialist training is necessary for those who wish to work effectively in this field and who wish to support and advise colleagues who, with increasing integration policies, will encounter children with speech and language disorders in their mainstream classrooms. If, as is estimated (AFASIC, 1989), one child in twenty in primary schools and one in eighty in secondary schools is affected by serious language disorder, education authorities should not ignore the needs of the children or their teachers.

REFERENCES

AFASIC (1989) *Breaking Down The Communication Barrier*, London: AFASIC.
——(1991) *AFASIC Checklists*, Wisbech, Cambridge: LDA.
Armstrong, F., Donlan, C., Halliday, P., Muskett, K. and Palmer, G. (1991) *Curriculum Requirement, Access And Recording* (Distance learning course for teachers of children with speech and language disorders), Birmingham: The University of Birmingham.
Barrs, M., Ellis, S., Hester, H. and Thomas, A. (1988) *The Primary Language Record*, London: Centre for Language in Primary Education.
Bishop, D. V. M. (1987) 'The causes of specific language disorder (developmental dysphasia)', *Journal of Child Psychology and Psychiatry*, 28, 1, 1–6.
Bishop, D. V. M. and Edmundson, A. (1986) 'Is otitis media a cause of specific developmental language disorders?', *British Journal of Disorders of Communication*, 21, 3, 321–38.
Bloom, L. and Lahey, M. (1978) *Language Development and Language Disorders*, New York: Wiley.
Byers-Brown, B. and Edwards, M. (1989) *Developmental Disorders Of Language*, London: Whurr.
Conti-Ramsden, G. (1987) 'Mother–child talk with language impaired children', *Proceedings, First International Symposium, Specific Speech and Language disorders in children*, University of Reading.
Crystal, D. (1988) *Introduction to Language Pathology* (2nd edn), London: Whurr.
Dalton, P. and Hardcastle, W. J. (1989) *Disorders of Fluency* (2nd edn), London: Whurr.
Davis, H., Stroud, A. and Green, L. (1988) 'The maternal language environment of children with language delay', *British Journal of Disorders of Communication*, 23, 3, 253–66.
Dewart, H. and Summers, S. (1988) *The Pragmatics Profile of Early Communication Skills*, Windsor: NFER-Nelson.

Donlan, C. and Hutt, E. (1991) 'Teaching maths to young children with language disorders', in K. Durkin and B. Shire (eds) *Language in Mathematical Education*, Milton Keynes: Open University Press.

Hutt, E. (1986) *Teaching Language-Disordered Children*, London: Edward Arnold.

Lahey, M. (1988) *Language Disorders and Language Development*, New York: Macmillan.

Miller, C. (1991) *Final Report to the Department of Education and Science: Project to Develop a Distance-learning Course for Teachers of Children With Speech and Language Disorders*, Birmingham: The University of Birmingham /Department of Education and Science.

National Oracy Project/National Curriculum Council (1991) *Teaching Talking and Learning in Key Stage 1/2/3*, York: National Curriculum Council.

Stackhouse, J. (1989) 'Relationship between spoken and written language disorders', in K. Mogford and J. Sadler (eds) *Child Language Disability*, Clevedon: Multilingual Matters.

Stackhouse, J. and Miller, C. (1990) *The Nature of Speech and Language Problems in Children* (Distance learning course for teachers of children with speech and language disorders), Birmingham: The University of Birmingham.

Stevenson, J., Richman, N. and Graham, P. (1985) 'Behaviour problems and language abilities at three years and behavioural deviance at eight years', *Journal of Child Psychology and Psychiatry*, 26, 215–30.

Webster, A. and McConnell, C. (1987) *Special Needs in Ordinary Schools: Children with Speech and Language Difficulties*, London: Cassell.

Wilson, D. K. (1987) *Voice Problems of Children* (3rd edn), Baltimore: Williams and Wilkins.

Useful addresses

Association for All Speech Impaired Children,
347 Central Markets,
Smithfield, London EC1A 9NH

The College of Speech and Language Therapists,
7 Bath Place,
Rivington Street,
London EC2A 3DR

6

EMOTIONAL AND BEHAVIOURAL DIFFICULTIES

Graham Upton

Roger is described by his form teacher as:

> a likeable boy but a major behaviour problem. He has been
> frequently absent from school over the past two years and
> when he is at school rarely turns up for lessons on time. He
> displays little interest in his school work and is steadily falling
> further and further behind his peers in all of the core subjects.
> He is disruptive in class and frequently talks inappropriately
> and out of turn. When reprimanded, he can become verbally
> abusive and has walked out of class on more than one
> occasion.

Such behaviour clearly affects the teacher's ability to create an
effective learning environment and, not unreasonably, this teacher
viewed Roger's behaviour negatively. In fact, the above statement
was made as part of an argument which had been put forward for
Roger to be excluded from his comprehensive school and placed in
a special unit for 'disruptive' pupils. While the above assessment of
Roger's behaviour was shared by most of his teachers, one
presented a different view. He wrote:

> I realise that most of my colleagues find Roger seriously
> disruptive in class. In fairness to Roger I think it is important
> for me to say that this is not the case in my subject. We have
> had our ups and downs but I feel now that I have established
> a positive relationship with him and he has not presented me
> with any disciplinary problems at all this year. His attainments
> were initially well below average for his teaching group but he
> has responded well to the system of individualised work
> sheets which our Department uses and while he is still in the

bottom group there is no problem with him working – he even asked to stay in during the lunch breaks this week to catch up work he had missed because of his recent truancy. I have also noticed a remarkable change in his attitude this year and he is very much more willing to acknowledge the problems he has in school than he used to be. I have had a number of long conversations with him of late and I think there is a lot of good in this lad if only we could harness it.

The experience of Roger which these two teachers report is strikingly different. Why should this be? Roger's own views expressed as answers to questions in an extract from an interview provide some insight into this apparent contradiction.

Interviewer: But, even when you come to school, from what your teachers say you are a bit of a problem in class. Why is that?
Roger: 'cause I hate school and I hate the teachers!
Interviewer: Why do you hate school and hate the teachers?
Roger: 'cause I can't do the work and the teachers don't try to help you. Most of them don't talk to you, they just bawl you out. And they don't listen either.
Interviewer: But I have also been told that you are doing all right in some subjects and that you do behave for some teachers.
Roger: Yeah, if they give you work that you can do and try and help you to catch up if you miss something then you behave, don't you. It's like . . . if they show you some respect then you respect them.

While most of Roger's teachers see Roger as the problem whose presence in their classrooms makes effective teaching and learning difficult it is clear that Roger has a different perspective on the situation. For Roger it would seem that it is ineffective teaching which makes learning difficult and prompts his 'bad' behaviour. But behaviour in school does not exist in isolation from the rest of the world and a further perspective on Roger is provided in an extract from a social work report.

That Roger is as well adjusted as he is, is surprising when we consider his family background. Roger is the eldest of six children who live with their mother and a 'stepfather'. Roger's father is currently serving an indefinite period in a secure psychiatric hospital as a result of a history of unpredictably violent behaviour towards members of his family and the general public. His 'stepfather' is well known to this office and he is currently involved in a Police investigation of child pornography and sexual abuse. His mother has a history of psychiatric disturbance and spent a period of six months in a psychiatric hospital soon after Roger was born, during which time Roger was placed in a foster home.

On the basis of this evidence, Roger's behaviour in school may be seen as reflecting a whole range of emotional conflicts to which family circumstances and experiences such as those described above may have given rise. So where does reality lie? In thinking about this there are a number of general points about the nature of emotional and behavioural problems which can be drawn from this example.

1   Perspectives on any emotional or behavioural problem can vary enormously. The differing views expressed in Roger's teachers' reports are contradictory but this does not mean that one is right and the other is wrong; Roger clearly relates differently with them and they with him and their understanding of Roger's behaviour reflects that.

2   Behaviour is frequently situation-specific and it is possible for someone to behave very differently in two similar situations as Roger does. The nature of the interaction between Roger and his teachers clearly resulted in very different behaviour being exhibited. It could probably be safely assumed that his behaviour at home is also very different to that at school.

3   Different teachers (and schools) have different standards for, and expectations of, the behaviour of their pupils. It is possible that the differences in Roger's behaviour reported by his two teachers may have reflected a greater degree of tolerance of difficult behaviour by the one who had fewer difficulties as much as any 'real' difference in Roger's behaviour.

4   Behaviour problems may be seen appropriately sometimes as discipline problems but further investigation sometimes reveals underlying emotional difficulties arising out of factors such as a difficult family background. Roger is undeniably a problem in class for most of his teachers but is he deliberately disruptive, as

his form teacher seems to believe; is he making a 'political statement' and protesting about poor teaching, as Roger himself suggests; is he reflecting models of behaviour which are the norm in his family but considered anti-social by society at large; or is Roger acting out a severe emotional difficulty whereby his behaviour in school is communicating the distress he has experienced as a result of the disturbing experiences of his family life?

WHO IS TO BLAME?

When trying to understand the occurrence of emotional and behavioural problems in schools there is a tendency, which is reflected in the views of Roger's form teacher, to assume that it is the pupils who are 'at fault'. This is true in relation even to the words that are used to describe such problems and to the way in which we have tried to understand the causes of such problems.

In this chapter the term '*emotional and behavioural difficulties*' has been used because it is currently the most commonly used term in Britain. The clear implication of this term, however, is that it is the pupils who have the emotional and behavioural difficulties; this is even more apparent in the popular abbreviation, '*ebd children*'. From 1944 to 1981 the official term which was used in Britain to refer to these children was 'maladjusted', which together with other terms such as 'disturbed', 'disruptive' and 'psychiatrically ill' suggests equally clearly that it is the child or young person who has, and is, the problem. Less formal terms, such as 'nutter', which tend to be used in the staffroom rather than formal terms such as those listed above, are perhaps even more direct in their attribution of responsibility.

While such conclusions often reflect a limited view of the situation, it is understandable that such a perspective may be adopted by teachers given their primary concern with establishing an effective teaching and learning environment in their classroom. The importance of this for teachers is reflected in the recently published report of the Elton Committee of Enquiry, which was set up specifically to enquire into disciplinary problems in schools and 'to consider what action can be taken . . . to secure the orderly atmosphere necessary in schools for effective teaching and learning to take place' (DES, 1989b, p. 11). It specifically rejects 'the view that bad behaviour is always entirely the fault of the pupil' and argues that

> Every incident has a range of immediate and longer term causes. Events in the classroom are influenced by a complex mixture of expectations, attitudes, regulations, policies and laws which are shaped by forces at work in the classroom, the school, the local community and society as a whole.
>
> (DES, 1989b, p. 64)

Nevertheless, it repeatedly refers to problem behaviour as bad behaviour. In fact, it is stated explicitly in the report that 'good behaviour makes effective teaching and learning possible. Bad behaviour disrupts these processes' (p. 57). In the light of Roger's comments about his behaviour in school it is interesting to note that the Elton Committee took no evidence from pupils. Researchers such as Reid (1985) and Cronk (1987), who have explored the perceptions held by disruptive pupils, have commonly found that they often view their acts of disruption as rational and justifiable responses to poor teaching. Unfortunately, not all teachers are perfect nor are they all working in schools which provide ideal learning environments where all pupils would assuredly learn if it were not for the disruptive influences of emotional and behavioural problems.

Alternative frameworks have been suggested to encompass a broader understanding of the issues and Galloway and Goodwin, for example, argue strongly in favour of the term 'disturbing'.

> By definition, children who are called maladjusted or disturbed attract these labels because they have disturbed adults. The adult's disturbance may be at the level of frustration or anxiety at not 'getting through to' the child, or it may be sheer physical fear of violence. The term 'disturbing' implies a recognition of the children's effects on adults while the terms maladjusted and disturbed are too often taken to imply psychological or social characteristics in the child.
>
> (Galloway and Goodwin, 1987, p. 15)

Such thinking recognises the importance of the different perspectives which exist in any situation and in Roger's case, for example, would highlight the importance of Roger's own views on the situation and the positive interaction which Roger enjoys with one teacher. Such a perspective also opens up the possibility of a behavioural problem being caused by participants other than the pupil and, in particular, forces us to look at the role which poor teaching may play in the genesis of such problems.

The term 'emotional and behavioural problems' is also seen by some as confusing because it blurs distinctions between what are arguably very different types of problems. Although there is clearly a connection between the areas of emotional difficulties and behavioural difficulties, they are not necessarily congruent. While not directly in its brief the Elton Report argues that a 'small minority of pupils have . . . severe and persistent behaviour problems as a result of emotional, psychological or neurological disturbance' (p. 150). Similarly, Circular 23/89 (DES, 1989c), which is intended to provide guidance about the nature of educational provision which Local Educational Authorities should make to meet the special educational needs of pupils with (*sic*) emotional and behavioural problems, presumably refers to this group rather than the full range of behaviour problems likely to be encountered in the ordinary classroom when it states:

> Emotional and behavioural difficulties are manifest in many different forms and severity of behaviour. Children with these difficulties exhibit unusual problems of adaptation to a range of physical, social and personal situations. They may set up barriers between themselves and their learning environment through inappropriate, aggressive, bizarre or withdrawn behaviour. Some children will have difficulty making sense of their environment because they have a severe pervasive developmental disorder or more rarely an adult type psychosis.
>
> (Para. 8, p. 3)

> Pupils with EBD are likely, by the time they enter a special school, to have developed a range of strategies for dealing with day-to-day experiences that are inappropriate and impede normal personal and social development, and make it difficult for them to learn.
>
> (Para. 10, p. 3)

In reality it is not as easy as these statements imply to distinguish between emotional disturbance and behavioural problems and the classification of children and young people as belonging to one or other of these categories is often more a matter of expediency than clinical assessment. Galloway *et al.* (1989), in arguing against the validity of this distinction, provide the following as evidence in support of their views:

> One of us (D.G.) has carried out a comprehensive assessment of well over 100 pupils following their exclusion from school and placement in off-site units for disruptive pupils. Without exception, all these pupils could have been described as having emotional and behavioural problems if a suitable special school had been available. Conversely, a high proportion of pupils placed in special schools could have been described as disruptive if an appropriate off-site unit had been available.
>
> (Galloway *et al.*, 1989, p. 101)

Following on from the above discussion of terminology it will come as no surprise to learn that attempts to explain the existence of emotional and behavioural difficulties in schools have, until recently, focused on what has been termed individual and family pathology. Thus, factors such as low social class background, poor housing conditions, disrupted parent–child relationships, parental disturbance and poor attainments, which are all evident in Roger's case, have been emphasised in identifying reasons why some children fail to respond positively to school. While not denying the significance of factors of this nature, researchers such as Rutter *et al.* (1979) and Reynolds (1984) have argued that schools and teachers also make a difference to the incidence of such problems.

It is not appropriate in this chapter to embark on a detailed discussion of these causative factors but it is important to note that generalisations about causes can help understand individual cases. At the same time it is equally important to recognise that individual problems can only be meaningfully understood by examining the circumstances surrounding that particular problem and coming to a reasoned conclusion about the interaction of the various influences that impinge upon it. In some situations an explanation based on events within the school or classroom may adequately explain the situation; in others a more complex analysis of events outside of the school and even going back into the pupil's early childhood experiences may be needed to make sense of things.

TACKLING THE PROBLEM

Underlying the differences of opinion about terminology and causation are major differences in the theories which have been advanced to account for their development and to provide a basis for intervention. At first glance these different approaches may appear contradictory but this is not necessarily the case and it is possible to draw from one or more of them in formulating a response which is appropriate to the difficulties that are presented and the situation in which they are to be addressed.

Behaviourism

In recent years behaviourism has tended to dominate attempts to understand and deal with emotional and behavioural difficulties in educational contexts. The ways in which behaviourism can be put into practice vary considerably (see, e.g. Wheldall, 1987) but the fundamental principles are simple.

1   The key concept is the notion that all behaviour, including unacceptable behaviour occurs because it is reinforced. Thus, in relation to a behavioural difficulty in school it is necessary to examine the classroom environment and the behaviour of the teachers and other pupils to determine how that behaviour is being reinforced. This is never easy and the suggestion that teachers may reinforce unacceptable behaviour patterns is one that many teachers find difficult to accept. Yet, teachers, even those in special schools and units, spend a large proportion of their time dealing with misbehaviour and a relatively small proportion of their time focusing on good behaviour. While the 'dealing with bad behaviour' might be done unpleasantly with the intention of stopping it, or tolerantly in order to communicate an understanding of the child's distress, the attention gained during these interactions can be reinforcing and paradoxically strengthen the very behaviour that it is intended to eliminate.

2   Second is the notion that maximal objectivity is essential particularly in defining and measuring the behaviour which is seen as problematic and the behaviour which is seen as desirable. General, and highly subjective, descriptions of behavioural difficulties such as 'frequently absent' and 'rarely turns up for lessons' as are made by Roger's teacher are not acceptable; rather a behaviourist would

want to know exactly how often Roger is away from school, which lessons he does turn up to and which ones he doesn't.

3 Finally, there is the assertion that it is possible to change behaviour by manipulating the consequences of the behaviour or changing the situation in which it occurs. Thus, ensuring a positive response from his teacher when Roger does attend his lessons may gradually lead to the development of a more regular attendance pattern. Equally, if we can see how a particular pattern of behaviour is being maintained then a simple solution to the problem can often be effected by changing the pattern of reinforcement. If, for example, we considered that Roger is 'disruptive in class' because of the teacher's attention which this produces, then withholding that attention may eliminate the problem. Or, if his lack of interest in school work reflects his inability to cope with the reading level of the worksheets and textbooks, then individualised worksheets might eliminate the difficulty, as indeed they appear to have done in the case of the one teacher who reported positively on him.

An analysis of a classroom situation using a behavioural framework can provide insights into the situation which can be used relatively informally or as a basis for the development of a behavioural intervention programme. On the formal level behaviourism offers a framework for general classroom management and school organisation within which the occurrence of emotional and behavioural problems can be minimised and an atmosphere created to foster positive behavioural development. Wheldall and Glynn (1989) describe an approach which is particularly relevant to whole class and whole school application in mainstream schools, while Burland (1987) looks at some of the specific issues involved in special educational settings. However, whatever the environment, the key to effective use lies in the concept of structure; structure that involves making clear the objectives which the school or class has for the behavioural development of its pupils and setting this within a framework which makes explicit the rules that govern the interaction between pupils and between teachers and pupils, and which provides clear and explicit motivation for pupils. With more extreme problems and in specialist settings such as special units and schools it is often considered necessary to implement formal behavioural change programmes. Normally, these are planned and undertaken with the support of someone with specialist knowledge of behavioural techniques such as an Educational Psychologist. However, an attraction of behavioural techniques is their simplicity and it is possible for a non-specialist to develop and use individualised programmes after a relatively modest amount of training. Over time a veritable armoury of more specialised and specific behavioural techniques has been developed and upon which the teacher can draw to deal with more extreme problems. It is not possible to discuss these within the constraints of this chapter but further details about specialised programmes and techniques can be found in Herbert (1987).

Dynamic psychotherapy

Dynamic psychotherapy provides us with a range of very different concepts and intervention techniques to behaviourism and in many ways constitutes the antithesis of all that is contained in behavioural theory and practice. While behaviourists focus on observable aspects of behaviour, objective measurement and the manipulation of external events in their attempts to understand and change patterns of behaviour, dynamic therapies are concerned with the inner world of feelings and emotions and seek to bring about change through deepening relationships and by helping the troubled individual to gain insight into the links between present events and previous experience. To many people, especially teachers, dynamic psychotherapy is seen as too specialised and esoteric to be of relevance to schools. In its pure form this is correct in that psychoanalytic training, for example, involves formal training and personal analysis over many years while psychoanalytic treatment involves daily sessions also normally over several years. The theory is highly sophisticated and its traditional techniques unsuited for classroom application. Nonetheless, some special residential schools (see, e.g. Reeves, 1983) have constructed therapeutic environments based on the principles of dynamic psychotherapy and it is also possible to utilise the basic principles of the approach in more rudimentary ways than are required in its purest application. Brown and Pedder (1979) provide a most readable summary of psychodynamic thinking and in the course of this discuss the possibility of therapy taking place at levels other than that of in-depth analysis. Within the framework they advance the key to dynamic psychotherapy at whatever level is the quality of the relationship between the 'therapist' and the 'client'. Above all this must be one of trust in which the client feels accepted by the therapist and able to engage in honest and direct communication; this will gradually lead to a growing understanding of the underlying distress and dis-ease. Within their framework they argue that therapeutic interaction can, and does, take place even in informal situations and the comments made by the teacher who reported positively on Roger could be taken to suggest that this relationship was one which had therapeutic potential.

A practical application of these ideas on a very basic level was popular in the 1960s under the title of 'life-space interviewing' and anyone interested in pursuing this line of thought will find much in a classic volume by Redl (1966) which has relevance to schools in the 1990s. Counselling is also an approach which owes much to the psychodynamic tradition although it had its immediate origins in humanistic psychology. Based on the work of people like Carl Rogers, counselling came to be seen in the 1960s and 1970s as central to the ability of mainstream schools to cope with the diverse emotional problems presented by their pupils (see Hamblin, 1978) but, more recently, its principles have been incorporated into general thinking about pastoral care (see Best *et al.*, 1983) and personal and social education (see Galloway, 1990). Group work techniques derived from this theoretical background have also significantly influenced therapeutic practice in special schools (see Lennox, 1982).

Systemic approaches

A common thread which permeates much contemporary thinking about emotional and behavioural problems in schools is that such behaviour is most fruitfully understood in the context of the situation in which it occurs. As noted above, recent research has suggested that pupil behaviour is often a function of teacher behaviour and that if teachers wish to change the behaviour of their pupils they need to consider whether it is in any way a product of the environment which exists in the classroom and school and may have to look hard at their own behaviour. It is also the case that pupils and teachers do not come to school devoid of emotional experiences or without established patterns of behaviour; how pupils and teachers behave in school and interact with one another will inevitably reflect those experiences and response patterns.

The interactive nature of behavioural patterns is recognised in behavioural and psychodynamic theories but distinct 'systemic' theories have been advanced. Cooper and Upton (1990) outline the features of one with immediate relevance to education. This is the *ecosystemic approach*, which seeks to understand emotional and behavioural problems in schools in terms of the interactions of the persons involved, either within the school situation or in related contexts (such as the family of the pupil concerned, the staff group etc.). From this perspective the following conclusions might be drawn about Roger's case:

1 The problem behaviour of which the form teacher complains does not originate from within Roger but from within the interaction between Roger and his teachers; a point which is well illustrated by the fact that one teacher does not experience difficulties with him. From the ecosystemic perspective, both Roger and his teachers have a rational basis for behaving in the way they do but they appear to be locked in a circular chain of increasingly negative interaction from which neither can readily escape – the more Roger misbehaves, the more negative his teachers become, the more negative they become, the more Roger misbehaves.

2 The circular nature of interactional patterns of this kind means that it is not appropriate to think of them in cause–effect terms. Roger's behaviour is undoubtedly problematic and his teachers are undeniably negative about his behaviour, but each can be seen, and indeed is seen by the different parties, as the cause of the other. Whether we *blame* Roger or his teachers depends on where we decide to *punctuate* the chain of events.

3 It follows from this, that intervention can be effectively achieved at any point in the system. If the pattern is circular the circle can be broken at any point and a change in Roger's behaviour will necessitate change in his teacher's behaviour and vice versa. As noted above in relation to the behavioural approach, such thinking is not necessarily easy for teachers to accept; recognising one's contribution to a problem situation is never comfortable but it does, for example, suggest other solutions in Roger's case than the present recommendation that he is excluded from

school and placed in a special unit. Within an ecosystemic approach it could be suggested that Roger's teacher needs to develop a more empathic under- standing of Roger's behaviour as a means of gaining a critical insight into his own behaviour.

There are many specific ways in which such an approach can be applied in relation to school-based problems. Readers interested in knowing more about this approach will find a useful elaboration of techniques which have particular relevance for classroom use in Molnar and Lindquist (1989) while those who are interested in the way in which schools and families can be brought together in effective intervention programmes can refer to Dowling and Osborne (1988).

WHAT SPECIAL EDUCATIONAL PROVISIONS ARE THERE TO HELP DEAL WITH THESE PROBLEMS?

The majority of children who present emotional and behavioural difficulties are in ordinary classes in ordinary schools. For the most part it is fair to say that teachers are effectively *on their own* in responding to such problems and generally do so on the basis of their own experience and in relation to the general ethos of the school. Schools rarely have clearly defined policies on emotional and behavioural difficulties although most have established disciplinary procedures and secondary schools tend to have formal pastoral care systems which govern the range of responses which are available to teachers. Following the publication of the Elton Report there has been increased pressure on schools to develop and adopt more consistent school policies and to ensure that school practices reflect these policies. There has also been an increasing focus on support for teachers rather than direct intervention with pupils and the role of Educational Psychologists in this has been reinforced in many Authorities by the creation of Behaviour Support Teams. The aim of these teams generally has been to assist the ordinary class teacher to understand and respond adequately to the problems which they are facing without taking away their responsibility for dealing with them. This is in contrast to the proliferation of special units and classes in ordinary schools in earlier years which all too often acted as dumping grounds for those children identified as disruptive.

Special educational provision is also made for children who present emotional and behavioural difficulties. Maladjustment was an official category of handicap under the 1944 Education Act and to cater for children and young people so classified a range of day schools and units and residential schools was established by Local Authorities and by private organisations and individuals. The 1981 Education Act abolished this system of categorisation and introduced a concept of special educational provision based on the special educational needs of individual children. While special educational needs are defined in terms of learning difficulties, emotional and behavioural difficulties are seen as coming within Section 2 of the Act, which refers to the existence of 'a disability which either prevents or hinders him (*sic*) from making use of educational facilities of a kind generally provided in schools within the area of the local authority' and special provision continues to be made for this group of children on this basis. In order for a pupil to be placed in a special school or unit on the basis of an emotional or behavioural difficulty a statement must be made under the terms of the 1981 Education Act confirming that the proposed placement is appropriate. *In theory* there is a wide range of provision available to meet the diversity of problems which are likely to be identified using these procedures. Special day schools and units exist, which ostensibly cater for those pupils whose problems are seen as primarily educational and where home circumstances are at least not unresponsive to help; special residential schools exist to deal with more severe problems where the problem is conceived primarily in terms of family difficulties and where it is felt that the pupil cannot be effectively helped while remaining in regular contact with his or her family; and a small number of hospital and psychiatric units provide day and sometimes residential care as an adjunct to psychiatric treatment. *In practice*, placement is more often determined by the availability of a place and the costs of the placement and, as noted by Galloway *et al.* above, it is frequently impossible to distinguish between pupils placed in these different sorts of provision.

Prior to 1981 this type of special educational provision was seen as primarily *therapeutic* with special schools commonly referred to as 'therapeutic communities'. Since 1981 there has been a growing emphasis on their educational functions; a trend which has been accelerated by the publication of an HMI survey of special schools and units for pupils with emotional and behavioural difficulties (DES, 1989a) which criticised them for not providing a curriculum of sufficient depth and breadth to meet the requirements of the National Curriculum. Therapeutic approaches have also been challenged by those who see the presenting difficulties more in terms of disciplinary problems. The Elton Committee which was referred to above concluded that many of the problems encountered by teachers can be remedied through the implementation of whole school approaches to discipline and the training of teachers in classroom management skills. While such suggestions have value in mainstream schools their relevance in more specialised settings is probably marginal. As is apparent in Roger's case, equating behaviour problems with issues of management and control is to ignore any underlying difficulty and other contributory factors and may have resulted in an escalation of the problem behaviour.

CONCLUSION

It would be nice to conclude this chapter with an account of a positive resolution of Roger's case. Unfortunately this is not possible. When the reports which were cited at the beginning of this chapter were written Roger was 15; no action was taken on the suggestion that he should be placed in a special unit, no special help was provided otherwise and his relationships with his teachers continued to deteriorate; during the year leading up to his sixteenth birthday he was rarely seen at school. Nothing is known of his subsequent life.

In Roger's case no simple solution was possible but intervention could have been initiated in a number of ways.

1   Fundamental to Roger's problem in school was his relationships with his teachers. Whether or not it would have eliminated entirely the problems about which his teachers were complaining, positive attitudes on the part of his teachers and efficiently managed classrooms where his learning difficulties were addressed could have helped to minimise the extent of this problematic interaction.

2   While one teacher appeared to have successfully created such a positive environment for Roger the others had not; if this teacher could have shared his understanding of Roger more effectively with his colleagues the magnitude of the problem surrounding

Roger may have been greatly diminished. Effective communication within a school can help teachers to help one another.

3   Specialist support could have been beneficial in helping the teachers to develop appropriate management techniques and specialised therapeutic management programmes and by providing advice on setting appropriate learning tasks and finding suitable curriculum materials. Help is usually available if it is sought.

4   If, at the end of the day, it had been accepted that his present school could no longer cope, his needs may have been more adequately met in a special educational placement. An ideal referral may have been to a special unit from which contact could have been maintained with the mainstream school; this can facilitate subsequent re-integration where that is realistic. Alternatively, a special day or residential school could have provided him with space and support to mature and overcome his learning difficulties.

5   Irrespective of what was done educationally some form of individual therapeutic help may have helped Roger while intervention in Roger's family was probably also called for given his family circumstances. While there is much that is within the power of schools to achieve it is equally important to recognise the limitations of teacher training and expertise. In situations where it is suspected that 'disturbed' behaviour may reflect 'disturbed experiences' referral to other agencies is of vital importance.

If even the most basic of this help had been provided it is possible that Roger would have left school with a more positive attitude towards himself, towards education and towards society in general. Emotional and behavioural problems provide a very different challenge to schools than the other handicapping conditions which are addressed elsewhere in this book. Because their origins are not always clear and because they are by nature disruptive to normal classroom routines they are rarely viewed sympathetically and all too often not even the most basic steps are taken to understand the difficulties which children and young people display. As in Roger's case, there are often complexities evident in instances of emotional and behavioural difficulties which it would be unwise for a teacher to try to untangle, yet there is also much, as his one teacher demonstrated, which can be understood with a little common sense and dealt with by means of goodwill and good teaching.

REFERENCES

Best, R., Ribbins, P., Jarvis, C. with Oddy, D. (1983) *Education and Care*, London: Heinemann.

Brown, D. and Pedder, J. (1979) *Introduction to Psychotherapy*, London: Tavistock.

Burland, R. (1987) 'The behavioural approach at Chelfham Mill School for Emotionally Disturbed Boys', in K. Wheldall (ed.) *The Behaviourist in the Classroom*, London: Allen and Unwin.

Cooper, P. and Upton, G. (1990) 'An ecosystemic approach to emotional and behavioural difficulties in schools', *Educational Psychology*, 10, 4, 301–21.

Cronk, K. (1987) *Teacher–Pupil Conflict in Secondary Schools*, Lewes: Falmer Press.

DES (1989a) *A Survey of Provision for Pupils with Emotional/Behavioural Difficulties in Maintained Special Schools and Units*, London: Department of Education and Science.

——(1989b) *Discipline in Schools: Report of the Committee of Enquiry Chaired by Lord Elton*, London: HMSO.

——(1989c) *Special Schools for Pupils with Emotional and Behavioural Difficulties*, Circular 23/89, London: HMSO.

Dowling, E. and Taylor, D. (1988) *The Family and the School: A Joint Systems Approach to Problems with Children*, London: Routledge and Kegan Paul.

Galloway, D. (1990) *Pupil Welfare and Counselling*, Harlow: Longman.

Galloway, D. and Goodwin, C. (1987) *The Education of Disturbing Children*, Harlow: Longman.

Galloway, D., Mortimore, P. and Tutt, N. (1989) 'Enquiry into discipline in schools', in N. Jones (ed.) *School Management and Pupil Behaviour*, London: Falmer Press.

Hamblin, D. (1978) *The Teacher and Counselling*, Oxford: Basil Blackwell.

Herbert, M. (1987) *Behavioural Treatment of Children with Problems*, London: Academic Press.

Jones, A. (1986) *Counselling Adolescents: School and After,* London: Kogan Page.

Lennox, D. (1982) *Residential Group Therapy for Children*, London: Tavistock.

Molnar, A. and Lindquist, B. (1989) *Changing Problem Behaviour in Schools*, San Francisco: Jossey Bass.

Redl, F. (1966) *When We Deal With Children*, New York: Free Press.

Reeves, C. (1983) 'Maladjustment: psychodynamic theory and the role of therapeutic education in a residential setting', *Maladjustment and Therapeutic Education*, 1, 2, 25–31.

Reid, K. (1985) *Truancy and School Absenteeism*, London: Hodder & Stoughton.

Reynolds, D. (1984) 'The school for vandals: a sociological portrait of the disaffection prone school', in N. Frude and H. Gault (eds) *Disruptive Behaviour in Schools*, Chichester: Wiley.

Rutter, M., Maugham, B., Mortimore, P. and Ouston, J. (1979) *Fifteen Thousand Hours: Secondary Schools and their Effects on Children,* London: Open Books.

Wheldall, K. (1987) *The Behaviourist in the Classroom,* London: Allen & Unwin.

Wheldall, K. and Glynn, T. (1989) *Effective Classroom Learning,* Oxford: Blackwell.

7

VISUAL IMPAIRMENTS

Heather Mason

INTRODUCTION

Following the publication of the Vernon Report (1972), the Warnock Report in 1978 and the Education Act 1981, educational provision in Britain for the visually impaired has undergone major changes. The Warnock Report acknowledged that children with sensory impairments frequently have special educational needs and that these can be met by providing a range of educational support for them. For instance, some children may always need the security of the 'special' school while others may have their needs met by being supported in mainstream by either a full-time teacher or a non teaching assistant or perhaps in a unit attached to a mainstream school. The Warnock Committee also recommended that the categories of visual impairment, blindness and partial sight, along with other categories of handicap, were no longer relevant as other 'educational' factors were far more important in relation to the educational placement of such children.

Since the 1980s, as a result of the legislation of the 1981 Education Act, falling school rolls and a decrease in the number of visually impaired children being born, many special schools for the blind and partially sighted have either closed or amalgamated their resources. A good example is the RNIB New College Worcester, which was formed from a residential girls 'grammar' school, and a similar one for boys. Both these schools had a tradition of academic excellence, with many pupils going on to university, but the new college is able to offer a greater range of subjects and activities. Some schools have changed the type of children they admit and are now facing the challenge of children with 'additional' difficulties

111

and at the same time providing a full, balanced and relevant curriculum for every pupil. All schools now have a full continuum of visual impairment as it is accepted that there is no clear dividing line between those children who are blind and those who have some vision. The nature of some of the remaining special schools has changed in other ways. For example, the high cost of residential education has meant that many schools now have Monday to Friday boarding only while others have diversified in other directions. Three good examples of this would be the development of further education and vocational courses, assessment centres for pre-school children and the school acting as a resource base for the peripatetic/advisory staff to support pupils in mainstream schools. Many schools, which were traditionally 'all age' schools, have now become either primary or secondary schools although in some parts of the country the original pattern remains.

Since September 1989, all teachers of children working in schools for the visually impaired in England and Wales have to take a course of training which is recognised by the Department of Education and Science (DES, 1989). Unfortunately, these regulations do not extend to those in a supportive or advisory role although many of these teachers are in fact qualified as teachers of the visually impaired. This qualification is needed by those teachers who contribute to the 'Statement of Special Educational Needs'.

Financial constraints as well as the philosophical debate on the merits of integration have resulted in many Local Educational Authorities setting up some kind of provision for the visually impaired within their own boundaries rather than sending children to special schools in other LEAs. This provision has been characterised by a rapid growth in the peripatetic/advisory/visiting teacher services for the visually impaired and by the setting up of units attached to both primary and secondary schools to act as resource bases for fully or partly integrated pupils.

A long established Visiting Teacher Service based at a special school for the visually impaired in Manchester works closely with all the mainstream schools where there may be children integrated and with the primary and secondary units attached to mainstream schools which have been developed to provide a wide range of resources and support. They also provide some support for neighbouring LEAs. This service sees their main functions in providing support to mainstream schools as 'offering help to classroom teachers, specialist assessment and teaching of children, the provision of resource materials, and In-Service training' (p. 10). This means that the service goes into mainstream schools and provides support in the following ways:

- explaining the effects of visual impairment and how it can affect the child's daily functioning;
- assessing the child's needs and advising the class teacher on setting objectives and planning programmes;
- advising on classroom placements and lighting conditions;
- working with the child, teachers, parents and other agencies involved;
- assessing visual functioning and providing training in the use of residual vision and co-ordination with the other senses;
- monitoring visual conditions and if necessary, referral to other agencies, e.g. Low Vision Clinic;
- training in the use of real and abstract forms to help with visual discrimination and perception;
- developing tactile and other sensory skills to complement vision;
- increasing short- and long-term memory skills;
- helping with self organisation;
- developing communication skills including listening, reading, spelling, handwriting and keyboard skills;
- helping with the acceptance of the impairment, self confidence and independence;
- helping with social skills;
- developing mobility skills;
- advising on resource materials for teachers and children – i.e. large print, raised work surfaces, low vision aids, personal computers; and
- providing In-Service training for teachers and staff.

This type of support which has acted as a model for other services has enabled an increasing number of severely visually impaired children to be integrated into mainstream schools. This can best be illustrated by the case of an academically able and highly motivated pupil now aged 17 and studying for three 'A' levels at a comprehensive school.

John has had cataracts from birth and spent his primary school years in a special school for the visually impaired. At the age of 12 he transferred to a mainstream secondary school mainly because of the wishes of his parents (one of whom also had cataracts), who were anxious that John should have the opportunity to take a full range of examination subjects at the age of 16. Fortunately, the teachers at the school were keen to take John and the Visiting Teacher Service provided awareness training for all the staff and for some of John's peer group and also some highly specific training relating to subject and classroom management. Full information was provided about the implications of John's visual impairment and resources were put into the school to enable access to the curriculum, e.g. photocopier with enlarging facilities, personal word processor and the services of a support teacher for three days a week. John was also provided with an intense programme of mobility training and study skills to enable him to become independent. Overall, the integration was a success apart from sporting activities where John had great difficulty in competing in team games but achieved success in swimming. He was very popular with his peer group and had no shortage of girl friends! While John was in the third year, it was decided that the school should develop a resource unit for pupils like John, permanently staffed by three qualified teachers of the visually impaired so that pupils could either integrate fully or partially into the mainstream with varying degrees of support.

ASSESSMENT OF INDIVIDUAL NEEDS

For children like John to be integrated into a mainstream school, a full assessment of their individual needs is essential so that the working environment can be planned and decisions made about what adaptations are needed, what additional skills the child needs to learn (e.g. mobility and orientation) and what is required in terms of technology to give access to the curriculum. Part of this assessment will include vital information relating to the actual visual disability and a typical profile (see figure 7.1) will include how the child sees, the medical information resulting from recognised tests for all aspects of visual acuity (the sharpness and clarity of vision) and the assessment of how the child is using his or her vision (often called 'functional vision').

Near and distance vision would be tested with the child using their prescribed spectacles or low vision aid so that a comparison can be made as to how their vision could be improved. If a child has

Visual condition and prognosis

Visual acuity   (i) distance vision   (ii) near vision

Recorded field defects

Colour vision

Preferred/dominant eye

Prescribed low vision aids

Appropriate lighting levels

Preferred print size

Additional impairments

Restrictions on physical activity

Medication

Figure 7.1: Profile of visual information

a severe visual impairment, then it is unlikely that spectacles will improve their vision to normally accepted levels; for some children, no benefit will be gained from wearing spectacles.

Good near visual acuity is needed for tasks such as reading, writing and other close work. The field of vision represents the total area the child can see when looking straight ahead; severely reduced visual fields result in 'tunnel vision', a characteristic of some eye defects (e.g. retinitis pigmentosa). While loss of colour perception is most common in the red/green part of the spectrum in about 8 per cent of all boys with normal vision, a rarer type of loss may also include blue/yellow deficiency. Problems will occur when access to the curriculum is through coloured apparatus and when activities require a high level of colour discrimination.

Functional vision

Alongside all the information gained from clinical tests, the teacher will want to know how the child uses his or her vision in and outside the classroom both in academic and non-academic and social activities. The use of vision will depend on factors such as the personality of the child but the teacher can build up the profile by observing them in different working situations and at different times of the day and keeping a record of the observations. It will also be necessary to assess certain areas of functioning, one of the most important being the development of visual perceptual skills and this can be done for younger children by using the *Look and Think* programme (Tobin *et al.*, 1978).

WHAT CAUSES A VISUAL IMPAIRMENT?

Many eye conditions are hereditary and can be passed to the child through either one parent carrying the relevant gene or in some cases where both parents are carriers. Unfortunately, parents may not have been aware that they carried the gene, so the birth of their child with a visual impairment will have been a major shock for them. In some societies, it is common for first cousins or other close 'blood' relatives to marry and this increases the chances of the eye conditions and any other impairments being passed on; it is important that genetic counselling is made available to these parents and, of course, to their children before they leave school. Other conditions may arise during the development of the foetus, some unexplained and some through infection (e.g. rubella). During the process of birth there is always the possibility of trauma, and for premature births where the birth weight is less than 1300 grams and where high levels of oxygen are required to sustain life, there is the high possibility of a condition known as retinopathy of prematurity occurring. During the first few years of life, there is the risk that illness can result in a visual impairment (e.g. brain tumours, viral infections) and children and young people are always at risk from road and other types of accidents. Unfortunately, some drug treatments for other conditions may also affect eyesight and in some countries, diseases spread by insects (e.g. flies carrying Trachoma), unhygienic conditions compounded by general poor primary health care and diet deficiencies are a major cause of visual impairment (Dobree and Boulter, 1982).

The three most common conditions which teachers in mainstream schools will come across are myopia (short-sightedness), hypermetropia (long-sightedness) and astigmatism. Most children with these conditions wear spectacles or contact lenses and their vision will be corrected to normal vision. Problems only arise if the spectacles are not worn for the purpose for which they were prescribed (e.g. close work). Mainstream teachers will also meet children who may be registered as 'blind' and others as 'partially sighted' or 'low vision' children. While blindness does not necessarily mean total lack of sight, these children are likely to be learning through tactile methods; the other visually impaired children will use print as their medium of access to the curriculum.

IMPLICATIONS OF A VISUAL IMPAIRMENT

Developmental delays are experienced by many visually impaired children and the magnitude of these delays will depend upon the severity and age of onset of the impairment and the early concrete experiences of the child. A great deal of learning which can be classed as 'incidental' comes through the visual channels so this is denied to the visually impaired child. Concepts have to be built up slowly, and in carefully thought out steps, and may need to be presented in a variety of methods or experiences. These early experiences of the child are crucial along with the attitudes of the parents to the visual impairment. The 'overprotectiveness' of many parents can be a barrier to the independence and motivation of the child. This is why it is important for professional help, for example through the advisory teaching service to be given to the parents from the moment of diagnosis and for these children to attend pre-school playgroups.

CLASSROOM MANAGEMENT

There are common problems faced by teachers of visually impaired children and while solutions have been suggested it is not possible to be specific about the needs of all the children as they can vary tremendously from one child to another, even with the same visual condition. However, table 7.1 lists some of the more common eye conditions which mainstream teachers encounter and suggests some of the areas which should be addressed in terms of lighting and print size.

Lighting

A major problem for the visually impaired child is 'glare' which can come from a variety of sources, including dirty windows, sunlight reflected from high-gloss paper or from direct sunlight, especially during the winter months when the sun is at a low elevation in the

Table 7.1 Lighting and print requirements of common eye conditions

Eye condition	Bright light preferred	Dim light preferred	Good contrast required	Large print required
Albinism		*	*	*
Aniridia	*	*	*	
Aphakia	*		*	*
Buphthalmus		*	*	*
Cataract – central		*	*	*
Cataract – peripheral	*		*	*
Glaucoma		*	*	*
Hypermetropia			*	*
Macula degeneration	*		*	*
Myopia	*		*	*
Optic atrophy	*		*	*
Photophobia		*	*	
Retinitis pigmentosa		*	*	
Retinopathy of prematurity	*		*	*
Squint	*		*	*

sky. By experimenting with an angle-poise lamp, the optimum individual lighting levels for individual children can be worked out in a variety of situations within the classroom, for instance for practical activities or for reading.

Printed materials

Some visual conditions, especially those that affect the central field of vision, are helped by the print being enlarged, either by some form of magnification using a low vision aid, or by an enlarging photocopier. However, this is not as straightforward a matter as it may seem since careful attention has to be paid to the quality of print (i.e. the size, colour and contrast on the paper), the type of paper (e.g. glossy paper) and in some cases to the quantity of print presented to the child. This caution refers to textbooks of all kinds, computer printer copies, and duplicated or handwritten notes as it is pointless enlarging a poor copy because the faults are just magnified. A common mistake made by many teachers is to enlarge onto A3 paper. This size of paper is very difficult to handle, takes up a great deal of desk space, creates additional visual scanning problems and usually time is not wasted in adapting the enlarged copy so that it fits on to A4 paper.

Very glossy 'glare'-producing paper and books with print across the illustrations are best avoided if possible although this presents a problem if visually impaired children are going to have access to the same books as the rest of their fully sighted class. The poor visual scanning and tracking skills of many young visually impaired children will mean that they experience additional difficulties on pages where the text is divided by illustrations or where there are double columns of text on the same page. Blind children enjoy reading the same books as their friends and although there are some reading schemes which have been especially produced for blind children so that the braille code can be introduced in a logical way, these books do not provide the same motivation as many of the attractive and exciting reading books found in most mainstream schools. It is possible to provide a braille copy of the text to be put into these books but this has to be done by someone who has knowledge of the child's progress in learning the more sophisticated Level 2 of the braille code in which contractions and word signs are introduced: for example, the word 'the' can be spelt out letter by letter or it can be represented by one braille sign and the stage at which these contractions are introduced depends upon the braille 'readiness' of the individual pupil.

Page marker and reading windows may be especially helpful to children who find it difficult to focus on an individual word or line of print and movement from one line to the next. An important point to remember is that it will take children with visual impairments, both braille and print users, a great deal longer to read and write the same amount as their fully sighted peers and as a result it may be necessary to reduce the amount of reading/writing that is expected in the same time as the other pupils. Needless to say, the visually impaired child should not be expected to share a book, diagram or map during a lesson and for the blind child this would be impossible.

There is no doubt that the biggest barrier to the academic

progress of visually impaired children is the extra time it takes them to perform tasks like reading in comparison to their fully sighted peers. Time is often considered to be an important factor when assessing the ability of a child and many standardised tests (e.g. reading tests) have a speed component built into them. If any kind of standardised test is given to a visually impaired child, the result will be invalid if the test has only been standardised for the fully sighted population. For pupils taking external examinations at 16+ or 18+, special provision has to be negotiated well in advance for the extra time the young person will need to read the questions, for large print examination papers or for amanuensis. For other externally assessed tasks (e.g. the Standard Attainment Tasks (SATs)), many of the activities based on print have to be adapted so that the visually impaired child is not penalised in any way. For the blind child, it may be that some of the tasks, like handwriting, will prove to be impossible.

If a visually impaired child is taking internal school examinations, consideration must be given to all the environmental factors such as levels of lighting and special attention must be given to the quality and size of print of the examination paper and, most important of all, the child must be allowed extra time, the length of which will depend upon the degree of visual impairment and the amount of reading involved. As a rough guide-line, allow an extra third to half of the total time; for example, if the test lasts one hour, allow one hour twenty minutes to one hour thirty minutes. Remember also that some children may experience visual fatigue, especially during the latter part of the afternoon, and so may not always produce their best work. This is especially true of children using low vision aids.

The problems encountered by visually impaired pupils in processing printed or tactile information and responding in written form represents, perhaps, the biggest academic difference between them and the fully sighted and these differences increase with age (Mason and Tobin, 1986). When a large amount of note-taking is expected from pupils, for example as dictation or from the blackboard, it would be fairer to devise other methods for the visually impaired child to have access to the same information. This can be done by giving notes in advance to a resource teacher so that a suitable print or braille copy can be made or a 'buddy' system can be used in which a friend is assigned to make a neat carbon copy or allow their notes to be photocopied. Alternatively, notes can be said aloud as they are written on the board so that they can be tape recorded.

Seating arrangements

While it is obvious that visually impaired children will need to be near the front of the class, information regarding the exact nature of their problem is necessary so that they are given the most appropriate working position in the centre of the room or to the right or left of the teacher. Other impairments such as a hearing loss need also to be taken into account. Because of the unusual close working position of some children it is also necessary to encourage good postural habits by providing a desk of correct height with either an adjustable slanting lid or a book stand, and a chair which fits the height of the child and desk. They also need adequate storage space for their books and specialist equipment so that a tidy and methodical approach to work can be developed. The severely visually impaired child using braille needs a large storage area, as braille books are unusually large and awkward, and unfortunately braille paper used for note-taking and other written work does not come in the usual metric paper sizes, making it difficult to file. It is advisable to have some storage space which is lockable, as many of the low vision aids such as binoculars and other technological aids like laptop computers are very expensive and highly desirable objects! In Sweden this ergonomic approach of providing the correct type of furniture, low vision aid, technology and working environment is considered to be a right of the visually impaired (Braf, 1984).

Safety

The teacher of visually impaired children has to think of safety all the time, not only in the classroom but in any other situation, and must be able to anticipate dangerous situations before they cause an accident. The reaction time of these children is much slower than others and it is all too easy when a child is coping well, to underestimate potential problems (Fitt and Mason, 1986). Always make sure that the child is aware of the layout of the classroom and indeed the whole school area and point out possible hazards. The blind child will need to be guided around any changes which take place and it will also be necessary to instil into the fully sighted children the need for extra awareness in common-sense safety. For instance, in the classroom, school-bags or other objects cluttering the floor, electric cables trailing across the floor, tilted chairs or objects and displays at low level, locker doors or similar left open at head height are a danger to all pupils but especially to those with visual impairments (Chapman and Stone, 1988; Fitt and Mason, 1986). For those children with difficulties in adapting to changes in lighting levels, going from a brightly lit classroom into a dark corridor or flight of stairs is a potential hazard. These areas need to be well lit and the careful choice of decoration of a light matt colour with perhaps bands of strong darker colours used as a contrast for doors and for stair treads, etc. can improve safety and visibility for these pupils. Movement within other parts of the school needs to be monitored carefully, for instance in dining rooms especially if there is a cafeteria system. It is important that ways are found which are unobtrusive to help the pupil to be as independent as possible.

Although certain practical activities in some aspects of the curriculum (e.g. Science or P.E.) require specific safety considerations, there is no need to bar visually impaired children from these areas of experience. With careful forward planning and co-operation from pupils and staff, they should be able to take part safely in almost all the activities available to their sighted peers. Access to the curriculum should not be denied children because their needs are not fully understood. Playground activities can be frightening for younger children, as they may be unable to react quickly to fast-moving groups of children and objects such as footballs and the vigilance of staff to anticipate dangerous situations is essential.

The teaching situation

For some of the more severely visually impaired children, a blackboard may be of little use for note-taking and alternative methods have already been suggested. However, if a child can read the board with the assistance of a low vision distance aid, then try to make sure that the handwriting is of a size which can be easily read. It is useful to consider how the information is displayed on the board making sure that there is some logical order and that a good contrast is obtained by having a 'black', not grey, board with white chalk. White boards used with black pen are excellent, provided they are cleaned thoroughly before use; pale colours on these boards and also on overhead projector transparencies are very difficult for all children to read so should be avoided. Some children may want to walk up to the board to check the information; this usually requires the co-operation of the rest of the class as their view of the board may be blocked, and not all children are tolerant!

For demonstration purposes, allow the visually impaired child to stand by your side if possible. During such occasions, think carefully about the amount of verbal explanation which is given at each stage as so often actions in such cases take the place of a detailed explanation. Try to avoid standing with your back to the window, as glare and light may silhouette your demonstration and do not assume that children can see clearly, even if they say so, as most children are reluctant to draw attentions to their difficulties and of course, may not be aware of exactly what they should be seeing. A closed circuit TV (CCTV), which some visually impaired pupils may have to enlarge print, can be used very effectively for demonstrations. It is important to consider also the acoustic quality and background noise level of a classroom as following verbal instructions can be a strain for children if they cannot see your face clearly.

Teaching and learning aids

It is often necessary to use a variety of methods and approaches so that these children have the same access to the curriculum as their fully sighted peers. Some of these methods will be extremely simple but effective, while others may require expensive equipment such as talking balances in science. The importance of forward planning cannot be stressed too much as large print, tactile or adapted copies cannot be produced just before a lesson. There needs to be a planning session before engaging on a topic or area of the curriculum to consider all the implications of access for the visually impaired. For instance, the child who is blind will need a braille copy of any notes or texts to be used by the rest of the class or a tactile diagram. The production of tactile (raised) diagrams is a very time consuming and a highly skilled art; the exact replication of a printed diagram is rarely appropriate and modifications have to be made.

Writing materials

The use of soft 'lead' pencils with younger children needs to be avoided as they do not provide enough contrast. Felt tips, usually black on white or yellow paper, provide the best combination and while older children will be able to decide for themselves which type of paper they prefer to write on younger children may be helped by using bold lined paper (available in different widths from the Partially Sighted Society). In an ideal situation, visually impaired children should be taught to touch-type from a very early age, as many experience great difficulty in reading back their own handwriting or producing pieces of work which are of an acceptable standard both to them and to the teacher. The availability of a new generation of laptop computers, quiet printers and a range of software allowing different sized prints has made a tremendous difference to children working alongside their sighted peers. Voice synthesizers with ear phones also give the same access to the blind child. Before purchasing any such equipment, advice should be taken from an independent source such as the National Council for Educational Technology or the Royal National Institute for the Blind (see Useful Addresses).

Additional curriculum areas

Because of their visual impairment, some children need time to develop skills not necessarily needed by their sighted peers. Some of these additional skills (e.g. braille literacy) may need to be taught by specialists such as advisory teachers for the visually impaired or, in the case of mobility and orientation training, trained mobility officers. However, skills such as keyboard skills will usually form part of the Information Technology curriculum of all pupils from an early age. The training of listening skills is important in helping children to make efficient use of their hearing; essential for the recognition of environmental sounds which are important for mobility and orientation skills. These skills are also needed by pupils who use taped materials and it is possible to teach children to listen to speech which is spoken at a much faster rate than normal using a special tape recorder which is designed for this purpose. Teaching these skills may create timetable problems as time-slots may have to be acquired from other areas of the curriculum; it is important that this is done in a thoughtful way so that a balanced individual curriculum is achieved without children losing out in areas like sporting activities.

It is perhaps useful to consider mobility and orientation skills in a little more detail. These are a complex set of skills which have to be taught to children so that ultimately they can move safely and independently around their school environment and further afield. The difficulties experienced by the visually impaired in developing these skills are not fully appreciated by the sighted population as many of these skills which are picked up incidentally by most people through visual cues from a very early age, have to be taught to the visually impaired child. Many of these children may have been overprotected by their parents (Warren, 1984) and may have missed even simple experiences such as going into a shop, buying sweets and handling the money.

Safe and independent movement around school, unless the child is totally blind, can usually be achieved fairly quickly with the help of an advisory teacher, class teacher and fellow pupils. However, independent travel to and from school, and other major skills, must be taught by a trained mobility officer especially if it is necessary for the child to learn the long cane technique.

Blind children (or those lacking in confidence) may choose to use a sighted pupil or teacher-guide in unfamiliar surroundings, perhaps on a school visit for example. For ease and safety of movement, the child should hold the guide's upper arm, just above the elbow, so that the thumb is on the outside and the fingers are on the inside of the guide's arm. Holding their arms close to the body automatically positions the visually handicapped child one half step behind his guide. The Royal National Institute for the Blind produces a useful leaflet entitled *How to guide a blind person* and this should be essential reading for everyone including fellow pupils.

SOCIAL SKILLS

In a mainstream situation, a totally blind child may have difficulty in making lasting friendships, partly because a great deal of our communication with one another is non verbal and takes the form of 'body language' – for example, all the gestures we make to express surprise, anger, happiness, scorn, boredom, agreement and many more. It is also easy for the child's lack of gestures to be misinterpreted. In addition, there are difficulties for the visually impaired child entering a classroom, searching for their group of friends in the playground, and knowing when to join into a conversation or when to initiate one. They may have no way of telling if their conversation is of great interest to other people or if a person is anxious to move away. This type of social interaction may be painful for children, so ways must be found (for example through drama and other role playing activities) to develop these skills and self image so that they become more confident in such situations. Like their sighted peers, visually impaired young people need sensitive guidance and information on sex education and at some stage may need individual counselling, either informally or formally, to make sure that there are no anxieties. This is especially important during puberty when bodies are changing rapidly and hygiene may be a problem. What has to be avoided is the dependence of the child upon an adult as this can easily happen in a situation where the child is 'supported' in some way by a member of the teaching or non teaching staff almost to the exclusion of social integration within class groups.

THE FUTURE

There is a continuing need for the academic and social progress and the visual impairment of the child to be carefully monitored. This can be done by working closely with the specialist adviser and with the parents so that any major difficulties can be anticipated and appropriate strategies employed.

REFERENCES

Braf, P. G. (1984) *The Physical Environment and the Visually Impaired*, Bromma, Sweden: ICTA Information Centre.

Chapman, E. K. and Stone, J. (1988) *The Visually Handicapped Child in Your Classroom*, London: Cassell.

Department of Education and Science (1972) *Education of the Visually Handicapped* (The Vernon Report), London: HMSO.

——(1978) *Special Educational Needs* (The Warnock Report). London: HMSO.

——(1989) *The Education (Teachers) Regulations. Circular 18/89.*, *London: HMSO.*

Dobree, J. H. and Boulter, E. (1982) *Blindness and Visual Handicap – The Facts*, Oxford: Oxford University Press.

Fitt, R. A. and Mason, H. L. (1986) *Sensory Handicaps in School*, Stratford-upon-Avon: NCSE.

Manchester Service for the Visually Impaired (1990) *Guide-lines for Teachers*, Shawgrove School, Manchester.

Mason, H. L. and Tobin, M. J. (1986) 'Speed of information processing and the visually handicapped child', *British Journal of Special Education*, 13, 2, 67–70.

Royal National Institute for the Blind (1990) *How to Guide a Blind Person*, London: RNIB.

Tobin, M. J., Chapman, E. K., Tooze, F. H. and Moss, S. C. (1978) *Look and Think: Handbook for Teachers; Teachers' File* (Schools Council Project), London: RNIB.

Warren, D. H. (1984) *Blindness and Early Childhood Development*, New York: American Foundation for the Blind.

Useful journals

British Journal of Visual Impairment c/o South Regional Association for the Blind, 55 Eton Avenue, London NW3 3ET.

The New Beacon c/o Royal National Institute for the Blind, 224 Great Portland Street, London WIN 6AA.

Occulus c/o Partially Sighted Society, Queens Road, Doncaster DN1 2NX.

Useful addresses

Research Centre for the Education of the Visually Handicapped, The University of Birmingham, Edgbaston, Birmingham B15 2TT.

National Council for Educational Technology, The Science Park, The University of Warwick, Coventry.

8

HEARING IMPAIRMENTS

Brian Fraser

This chapter is concerned with the nature of hearing loss in children and is particularly addressed to the needs of hearing-impaired children in mainstream classes and to the educational sequelae of the condition. Such a chapter cannot adequately address all of the issues which are likely to be faced by the classroom teacher and so can only be regarded as the briefest introduction. More detail can be found in Webster and Ellwood (1985) and in Webster and Wood (1989).

The consequences of hearing losses in children are more far-reaching than is immediately apparent. Such losses interfere with the ability of children to exchange information with their environment and expose them to fewer experiences than are available to children with normal hearing. There are obvious difficulties in inter-personal communication, which at the extreme with untreated profound or sub-total hearing loss, can result in a complete inability to understand conventional language and a related inability to speak. Untreated conditions of such severity are unlikely to be met in the ordinary classroom but it is likely that most teachers will encounter children with less extreme but nevertheless, seriously handicapping language problems resulting from permanent, temporary or even intermittent losses of hearing of varying degrees of severity. Such hearing losses can cause delays in language development lasting for several months or several years. The consequence of language delay may create gaps in understanding which arise from failure to grasp linguistically based concepts associated with new learning. Speech may be affected by the inability to hear adequate models against which the spoken word can be monitored. The linguistic effects of hearing loss for a child in an ordinary classroom are grave

129

since most, if not all, schooling is dependent upon adequate comprehension of the spoken and written word. The written word itself cannot be an adequate substitute for the former as the ability to read is dependent upon the ability to communicate verbally – difficulty with the one skill will be reflected in poor attainments in the other.

The source of the language deficit does not lie solely in the hearing loss. Wood *et al.* (1986) have demonstrated that the patterns of language offered to the child are likely to have a major impact upon the level of linguistic development. Regardless of the source of the language deficit the effects are likely to be the same and can be threefold – cognitive, social and abstract (Fraser, 1990).

Language is the medium which is used for the categorisation and organisation of experiences in the social and material world. This is the cognitive function of language and as such it permits a fine and flexible system of categorisation in order that the relationships between things and people can be clearly organised.

The second function of language is concerned with the exchange of common elements of experience. This function relates to interpersonal communication and permits the easy exchange of experiences occurring at the present or having occurred in the past or anticipated as occurring in the future. This aspect of language promotes the development of the shared understandings which are essential for anyone to function in society (Newson, 1978). These shared understandings can be the private and excluding feelings and concepts enjoyed and practised within a family or other small community or they can be the wider understandings of a greater society which are contributed to by tradition and literature. Newson sees these as being the common reference points, the shared constructs, the sympathies, the ability to put oneself into the position of others and the reciprocal interactions that are all necessary for integration into any society.

The third function of language is that which relates to abstract experiences. It is through this function that feelings, emotions, moral and spiritual ideas and scientific and mathematical concepts can be expressed flexibly and precisely.

A child with limited language ability will have limitations imposed on each of these functions of language. Each will result in an inevitable reduction in the child's experiences.

Experiential limitation and an alteration in the nature and quality of experiences can also arise from other aspects of communication such as information which is non-linguistic but which signals changes in the environment. A person with hearing loss will be unaware of some sounds in the environment which for a person with normal hearing signify a need to alter behaviour or to accommodate the signalled change. A telephone bell ringing or a shout will cause most people to cease the immediate activity and attend to the new one which has been signalled auditorially. Hearing is used here at its most basic level, as a warning sense. Hearing is a mandatory sense and functions at all times. It only ceases to operate for physiological or psychological reasons. Unlike vision, the other sense concerned with information from a distance, hearing cannot be controlled. It cannot be switched off. Children with hearing losses will be denied many of the experiences to which they have not been alerted by the sense of hearing. The effect of this will be a reduction in the level of experience enjoyed by a person with normal hearing. The environment will also be very much less secure and potentially more frightening than that experienced by others.

A further aspect of the effect of hearing loss is that which relates to temporal sequencing. All auditory information is organised in time and is thus temporal information. Visual information is more spatial in character and allows opportunities for detailed scrutiny. In order to relate one sound to another and to interpret an auditory experience, such as spoken language (and even its visual representation, the written word) it is necessary to develop temporal sequencing skills. These skills allow for information occurring in time to be retained in the memory and for an interpretation of this to be made upon the completion of the whole message. For example, to interpret this sentence correctly, it is necessary to retain information from the beginning and to relate this to later information before reaching a conclusion on the meaning when the sentence finishes at the full stop. Understanding depends upon relating the message to information held in the long-term memory. The ability to handle information depends upon retaining that information in the short-term memory. Temporal sequencing skills are necessary for efficient functioning of short-term memory but the development of such skills is dependent upon the ability to hear, hearing being the principal sense for dealing with temporally organised information. Hearing loss will effect the development of temporal sequencing skills and this will have an effect on the ability to process and develop conventional language skills. The early detection of hearing loss and the early fitting of hearing aids to utilise residual hearing is an important factor in promoting the development of temporal sequencing skills in deaf children. The majority of hearing-impaired children found in mainstream schools will have had several years experience of amplified sound before entering school and will be in the process of developing such skills; this development will be enhanced by burgeoning verbal language development.

This introduction has highlighted the principal effects of hearing loss for children. It has focused upon the auditory condition in the child and as such has concentrated upon the deficit. Problems for the child are just as likely to arise from factors outside the child. The attitudes of parents, teachers and wider society can strongly influence the development of handicap in hearing-impaired children and in children with other impairments. The central effect of hearing impairment and the reaction of others to the loss, is one of limitation of the experiences which are necessary for optimum cognitive development, for the development of social skills, for the development of the ability to adapt and for the development of learning skills. It is not just in the limitation of language that the main effects of hearing impairment lie but in these areas also.

THE NATURE OF HEARING LOSS

The effects of different types of hearing loss depend upon the auditory condition. A loss of hearing as a result of the malfunctioning of the outer and middle ear system will be different from a loss caused by a defect in the inner ear – that part of the ear which contains the end organ of hearing. The outer and middle ear (the ear canal and the small cavity immediately behind the ear drum) conduct sound waves to the cochlea in the inner ear. The cochlea converts the sound waves into nerve impulses for transmission to the brain; it is the means by which different sound pitches and levels of intensity are perceived.

Cochlea mechanism hearing losses and losses caused by damage to the nerves are known as sensori-neural losses. These conditions tend to create the more severe or profound hearing losses and they are also not generally amenable to medical treatment. They can be caused by hereditary or disease conditions which affect the developing foetus, for example maternal rubella, or German measles contracted early in pregnancy (this potential cause of congenital deafness is now greatly diminished as a consequence of the introduction of vaccination programmes). Sensori-neural deafness can also be caused by diseases contracted during childhood, for example, meningitis and encephalitis.

It is generally the case that sensory neural losses do not affect all sounds equally. The ability to hear high-pitched sounds is often more seriously affected than that for low-pitched sounds. Thus, in addition to reduced ability to hear, a child with sensori-neural deafness will also be presented with a distorted version of the sound. At the extreme it is possible for a child to have normal or near normal hearing for low-pitched sounds and at the same time a profound loss for high-pitched sounds. The effects will be that the child hears most vowel sounds reasonably well and will appreciate the prosodic features of speech (the rhythm, intonation, stress and pause) but will be denied access to the important information-carrying consonants. The child with this type of deafness would give the superficial appearance of being able to hear – after all, if the child's name is spoken softly from behind there will be a response to those speech components that are audible. What such a child will not be able to do is to follow more complex language because of his or her inability to hear important high-frequency components. You can judge for yourself the difficulty involved by attempting to read and interpret the two nursery rhymes below. In the first all vowels are omitted but its sense is relatively unimpaired. In the other all consonants have been removed and interpretation is almost impossible.

H_mpt_ D_mpt_ s_t _n _ w_ll

H_mpt_ D_mpt_ h_d _ gr__t f_ll

_ i_ _e _a_ _or_er _a_ i_ a _or_er

ea_i__ _i_ __i__a_ _ie.

The addition of the clue that the second rhyme involves a boy enjoying a festive repast and at the same time inconsequently praising himself, goes some way to solving the problem.

It was suggested above that sensori-neural deafnesses are not amenable to medical treatment. This is not strictly true. A new technique is being used in children where the cochlea has to all intent been destroyed but the auditory nerve is retained intact. In such cases the resultant hearing loss is generally of the profoundest nature. A device known as a cochlea implant can be used with some children with this type of loss. This consists of a series of electronic channels which can be threaded into the non-functioning cochlea. The electronic signals from these channels are produced by processing sounds which are received in a microphone in a special instrument worn by the child. These signals are picked up by the auditory nerve and are transmitted to the auditory receptive areas of the brain. This system does not restore normal hearing but it may allow the child to have access to sound stimuli at the sort of level that would be enjoyed by a child with a slightly less profound hearing loss who is using conventional hearing aids. The signal is also very distorted.

The other form of hearing loss has its source in a malfunctioning of the outer or middle ear systems; those concerned with the conduction of the sound signal to the cochlea. Defects in these parts of the ear result in conductive deafness. Generally with conductive deafnesses the sensori-neural mechanisms would function properly if only the energy from the sound waves could reach them. It is, however, possible for a child with a sensori-neural hearing loss to develop a condition which adds a conductive deafness overlay to the already existing condition. Conductive deafnesses can be caused by blockages resulting from impacted wax in the outer ear or mucous in the middle ear. Disturbance of the conductive mechanism can also be caused by damage to the ear drum or by dislocation of the chain of three small bones which mechanically transmit sound energy from the ear drum to the cochlea. There are many reasons for breakdowns in this system but the most common in children are associated with upper respiratory tract infections such as the common cold, catarrh and tonsillitis. Most conductive hearing losses in children respond well to treatment but in some cases this may be lengthy. The effects of conductive deafness are generally less complicating than those of a sensori-neural type and are, in most cases, less severe and do not have the same distorting effect upon received sound. There is a more or less even dulling of sound but one which nevertheless makes listening a great effort and which can cause the child to lose attention. The hearing loss may also be intermittent, varying from day-to-day or week-to-week depending upon the child's state of health. The effects of this can be confusing for the child and can present the teacher with the impression of a child whose attention is far from consistent.

Conductive deafness is particularly prevalent during the early years of schooling. The reason for this is associated with the physical development of the child, particularly as this relates to the skull and to the tissues in the naso-pharynx. Young children in the infant school are particularly susceptible to middle ear conditions and it has been demonstrated that at any time as many as one such child in five has a middle ear condition likely to cause hearing loss in one ear or both. In most instances these conditions cure themselves spontaneously. In some cases the condition persists and requires some form of medical or surgical treatment in order to effect a cure. Generally the hearing loss is caused by a build-up of mucous in the middle ear cavity. This cavity is the space immediately behind the ear drum and it is linked to the naso-pharynx by a tube which opens on swallowing or yawning. The function of this tube is to replace air in the middle ear system – air pressure has to equal atmospheric air pressure if the ear drum and the associated chain of bones are to work effectively. The tube also allows any mucoid fluid in the middle ear to drain away. If this fluid cannot easily drain, perhaps because it has become infected and somewhat thick and sticky, then the middle ear system will not function properly. The presence of fluid in the middle ear will impede the transmission of sound energy in much the same way that water impedes the ability to walk easily in a swimming pool. The fluid can be removed by prescribing decongestants or, in some cases, by making an incision in the ear drum and sucking the glue-like substance out. Frequently, it is necessary to insert a tiny semi-permanent opening into the eardrum in order to aerate the middle ear and thus to facilitate the evacuation of fluid down the tube which communicates with the back of the throat. This opening is effected by the insertion of a very small tube known as a grommet into the ear drum. This procedure has proved to be particularly effective in reducing the auditory effects of middle ear conditions. The grommet rarely needs to stay in for more than about six months but during this time it must be remembered that the child has a hole in the ear drum and that activities such as swimming may not be possible.

Infection from enlarged tonsils or adenoids can sometimes spread into middle ear fluid causing pus to develop. The fluid is then likely to expand and create pressure in the middle ear cavity. This can be extremely painful and distressing. Such conditions are generally treated by the use of antibiotics but occasionally it is necessary to remove tonsils and adenoids.

Other conductive deafnesses can be caused by simple blockages of the external ear canal. A blockage of wax is sufficient to cause a marked difficulty in hearing. Wax normally flakes away naturally but occasionally it remains moist and can become impacted in the ear canal. Over-zealous use of cotton buds can push the wax inwards and cause a build-up. The ear moulds, with which hearing aids fit into ears, can also prevent the normal loss of wax. It is not uncommon for hearing aid users to have additional hearing loss created by a build-up of wax.

THE RECOGNITION OF HEARING LOSS IN CHILDREN

All local education authorities have arrangements for the medical examination of children in schools either once or several times during their educational careers. Most district health authorities which conduct these examinations have procedures for the screening of hearing usually starting long before children start school. It is unusual not to find facilities for the routine testing of hearing in babies from about 7 or 8 months of age and the vast majority of the more severe auditory conditions will have been detected and the children are likely to have been in the care of an educational service for hearing-impaired children for several years before formal schooling starts. When children start school there is generally a programme of screening tests of hearing designed to detect those children who may have been missed in earlier screening or who have developed auditory conditions subsequently. In some authorities such screening programmes are also repeated at later stages. Even with such regular screening it is still important that class teachers should be alert to possible signs of auditory deficiency. The Warnock Report (DES, 1978) stressed the importance of class teachers being able to recognise the early signs of special need and it is suggested that teachers should know how to identify conditions which indicate such need. Listed below is a list of signs and behaviours which could indicate auditory deficiency.

The following are idicators of hearing loss in children in mainstream classes:

- do not respond when called
- hear their name and simple instructions (particularly where situational cues are available) but little else
- misunderstand or 'ignore' instructions; frequently ask for repetitions
- watch faces closely (a child with even a quite mild hearing loss may depend upon watching the face of a speaker in order fully to comprehend the spoken message)
- frequently seek assistance from neighbours
- reluctant to speak freely, e.g. nod or shake head rather than saying 'yes' or 'no'
- speak very softly
- shout, or talk overly loudly
- appear dull
- appear disinterested
- appear withdrawn into a personal world
- inattentive
- display behaviour problems and poor social adjustment
- troublesome and naughty behaviour in the classroom (children may try to relieve boredom by worrying their neighbours)
- retardation in basic subjects, particularly in reading and verbal subjects
- low scores in dictation work and oral mental arithmetic but good results elsewhere
- persistent colds and catarrh
- complain of earache
- discharging ears
- speech defects
- deafness in parents or siblings.

Any child displaying one or more of these signs or behaviours should be referred for specific hearing testing as the first part of any investigating process.

If a child is suspected by the class teacher of having a hearing loss the child should be referred for further investigation but only after this has been discussed with the parents. The referral route is generally relatively straightforward. All local education authorities have a service for the education and support of hearing-impaired children in mainstream schools. This service will have strong links with medical facilities and will make arrangements for further investigations.

Assessment of hearing-impaired children is concerned with two aspects of their condition. The first involves the possibility of the cure or reduction of the hearing loss; the other with maximising personal and educational development. Assessment measures consider both clinical and functional aspects of the child and the hearing loss and the child receives a range of hearing tests which measure auditory acuity across a range of tones which span the frequencies of which speech sounds are composed. These tests result in a graph showing the quietest sounds to which the child responds. Such information showing the threshold of hearing are of use to audiologists and to ear, nose and throat consultants and assist in the making of decisions related to the fitting of hearing aids and any surgical intervention that may be needed. More important to the teacher are tests of functional hearing. These demonstrate what the child can do with the hearing that is available. Such tests should be conducted in different conditions and will show how the child responds to speech when the speaker is visible, when the child cannot see the face of the speaker, when the child is wearing hearing aids and probably how the child responds in different sound environments. Such examinations have obvious and important implications for classroom management and can form the basis for the discussions between the classroom teacher and the specialist visiting teacher of the deaf. Other components of auditory assessment are concerned with the possible source of the difficulty and the possibility of physical treatment of the condition.

In addition to the auditory assessment of the child it is also important that some sort of objective measure is made of the child's developmental needs. The restrictions on experience that have been described above can result in a seriously reduced level of attainment. An important component of this developmental assessment will relate to language.

HEARING-IMPAIRED CHILDREN AND THEIR EDUCATION

While it must be acknowledged that acute conductive deafness can cause serious problems for the child in school (Garner, 1985) and while it must be recognised that many, if not most children suffer from such conditions at some time during their pre-school or school years this part of this chapter will be restricted to children with sensori-neural hearing losses or with chronic conductive conditions – that is, to those with permanent or very long-term deafness.

The incidence of deafness varies considerably. Estimates suggest that about two children in every 1,000 will have a permanent deafness. This ratio is likely to fluctuate and there have been times when it has been very much higher – during the mid-1960s the incidence rose to nearly 3.8/1,000 as a consequence of two rubella epidemics in the first half of the decade. In 1989 there were known to be 15,701 children in Britain who were receiving educational help from teachers of the deaf. At least another 41,894 children in main-stream schools had variable conductive hearing losses or milder conditions that did not require regular support from a teacher of the deaf (BATOD, 1989). Of those children in school, 18 per cent were in special schools for hearing-impaired children, 17 per cent in units attached to mainstream schools, 53 per cent in mainstream classes and 12 per cent in other special schools. Most of this last group would have been children with other impairments. These figures show that 70 per cent of hearing-impaired children who were receiving educational support from a specialist teacher of the deaf were in the mainstream sector in one type of provision or another. This represents a major change in placement practice since as recently as thirty years ago when few places were available in the newly developing units for partially hearing children and when visiting specialist teacher services were in their infancy. Schools for hearing-impaired children were then more numerous and offered more places than is now the case. There are three main reasons for this change: early detection of hearing loss in babies, subsequent early utilisation of residual hearing by fitting appropriate hearing aids, and early educational intervention in the form of parent guidance programmes delivered by services for hearing-impaired children. The combined effect of these was that fewer hearing-impaired children at school entry age required the intensive interventions provided in schools for the deaf. Far more were able to take their place in the mainstream of education albeit with varying degrees of support. Units for hearing-impaired children never have been separate classes within mainstream schools; they have always promoted a degree of integration into normal classes with varying degrees of in-class and withdrawal support. Visiting teachers of the deaf have provided support for other children in mainstream classes which has varied from intensive programmes involving several visits each week to advisory visits to schools on a termly basis depending upon assessed need.

MODES OF COMMUNICATION

When integration programmes first began to accelerate in the early 1960s the prevailing language approach used with children was oral, with children being expected to speak and to understand conventional spoken language. Most of the children had moderate hearing losses and required little intensive language intervention. Since then there has been a development in interest in the use of different modes of communication, all of which have been used with hearing-impaired children in mainstream schools. The main systems in use have been outlined by Fraser (1990) while a more detailed account is provided by Lynas *et al.* (1988).

The modes of communication currently used in the education of hearing-impaired children fall into three main categories:

1 Oral
2 Sign Language
3 Total Communication

However, there is a difficulty in deciding where a particular approach should be assigned. Total Communication for example, is seen by some as essentially an oral approach while others may see the system that they operate as being more closely related to Sign Language. Those who see Sign as the 'natural' language of deaf people would argue that some systems of signing cannot properly be described as Sign Language.

Oral approaches

There are two main approaches to oral methods, the traditional oral and the oral/auditory.

Traditional oral

The emphasis here is upon the development of language through the use of lip-reading skills and a systemised approach to language teaching. Visual cues other than lip patterns are de-emphasised; it is assumed by the advocates of the approach that deaf children are unable to 'catch' language incidentally and as a result highly structured forms of language had to be taught and learned using contrived exercises similar to the traditional approaches used for teaching second languages (Andrews, 1988).

Auditory /oral

This approach is seen by some as a *laissez-faire* system in which nothing constructive appears to be happening apart from an insistence that the deaf child wears appropriate and carefully maintained hearing aids; there is apparently no attempt to teach language skills. This superficial appearance belies two underlying principles. The first relates to the use of residual hearing and the presumption is made that in all but very rare cases, deaf children have elements of residual hearing which can be utilised in the acquisition of spoken language. Early and consistent use of residual hearing will enable the child to develop listening experience which will facilitate the acquisition of the language experience and cognitive skills necessary for the interpretation of spoken language. The hearing aid, with correct use, becomes integral to the child's personality and indispensable. While the hearing aid cannot compensate for the hearing loss in the same way that spectacles can compensate for a visual deficiency it can provide elements of information in the complexity of signals which go to make up conventional language.

The second underlying principle relates to the nature of the language input provided and this is determined by the principles of normal language acquisition. It is argued that the usual interactions between children learning language and their parents are uniquely structured and that they facilitate language acquisition. The child brings to this interactional process a language acquisition ability and the adult brings language-enabling behaviours. Wood *et al.* (1986) have demonstrated that inappropriate interactional practices contribute more to language deficiency and deviance in hearing-impaired children than the hearing loss itself.

Sign Language

Sign Language is a language code based upon a manual system of arbitrary codes. In Britain it is generally known as British Sign Language, or BSL. This is a language in its own right and has no relationship to the spoken language of the wider community in that it has a different syntactic and organisational structure. It has been postulated that Sign is the natural language of deaf people and that deaf children should be educated in Sign as a first language. When fluency has been achieved then English can be taught as a second language. The educational approach then becomes bilingual. There are many attractions in this argument but there are also difficulties. As was pointed out above, the acquisition of language by children depends upon unique interactions between children and adults. This interaction is conversational with the adult adopting a linguistic register, which is contingent upon the developing needs of the child. To be able to make such an adjustment the adult must be fluent in the language. Very few adults are sufficiently fluent in Sign to be able to make such a register adjustment and this is unlikely to be achieved by an adult who is learning Sign as a second language. It is true that there are some deaf children born of deaf parents who themselves may use Sign in the home as their preferred language. However, only 3 per cent of deaf children have both parents who are deaf and only a further 7 per cent have one deaf parent and not all of these parents will be Sign users (Lynas *et al.*, 1988). If a deaf child is rapidly to develop Sign as a first language then there needs to be an intensive programme of Sign Language teaching to parents and to teachers so that they may acquire the linguistic fluency necessary for the appropriate register adjustments. This is not always realistic and an alternative is to use Sign users from the deaf community to provide appropriate input. This is in fact happening in some centres. Programmes of first language teaching in Sign are being tried but their outcomes are, as yet, uncertain and there is no evidence to show that a child exposed to such a programme will necessarily be in a better position later to acquire English.

Total Communication

Total Communication seeks to provide the child with as many sim-ultaneously delivered systems of access to language information as possible. The child is presented with language through oral, auditory, lip-read and signed support systems. The message is thus seen to be protected by some sort of communication overload (Fraser, 1990). English is the medium of instruction supported either by 'Signed English' or by 'Signs Supporting the English'. With Signed

English, signs are used which are based upon the vocabulary of British Sign Language but the signs are delivered according to the structure of English and are presented simultaneously with the spoken message. In Signs Supporting English spoken patterns are supported with key signs as appropriate but without attempting to replicate the verbal message completely in sign.

The research evidence that is beginning to emerge from the United States, where this system has been in use for more than a generation of schoolchildren, is not encouraging with children failing to acquire language in the accelerated way that had been anticipated (Lynas *et al.*, 1988). The research has demonstrated that even the best practitioners fail to communicate with complete spoken or manual messages and as a result the child is presented with a limited and incomplete linguistic input. Another factor to be considered is that the child is being presented with competing message systems and these could cause a cognitive overload which would encourage the child to concentrate on one system and not the others.

EDUCATIONAL MANAGEMENT OF HEARING-IMPAIRED CHILDREN IN MAINSTREAM SCHOOLS

In most cases the education of a child with impaired hearing in a mainstream class involves a partnership between the class teachers and a range of people including parents, specialist teachers, audiologists and medical specialists. In some cases other people such as social workers and interpreters may be involved also. Central to the partnership is the child and before processes of educational management can be initiated the needs of the child have to be determined by careful and comprehensive assessment. Clinical and functional aspects of the hearing loss will be determined by the audiologist and the specialist teacher of the deaf. The child will be given a range of hearing tests, an important aspect of which will be concerned with the way in which the child functions with normal speech and how the hearing loss can be aided by amplification. Such assessments have obvious and important implications for classroom management and should be discussed fully with the class teacher by the teacher of the deaf.

In addition to audiological tests it is also necessary to have some objective assessment of the child's development. The restrictions of experience described above can result in a seriously reduced level of attainment. Standardised tests may well confirm the impression of overall dullness. It is important to examine the child as broadly as possible and to make an assessment which is criterion referenced rather than one which is norm based – the latter approach is likely to distort the view of the child and will do the child a disservice by confirming surface and subjective views of the child's abilities and attainments.

An important element of formal assessment is that concerned with language. Many services for hearing-impaired children will make regular analyses of children's language, examining syntactic and pragmatic components. It is also important to analyse the language of the people who are interacting with the child as inappropriate input will contribute to delay in the acquisition of communication skills.

There is a great deal which is not measurable in formal terms and it is here that the observant and informed classroom teacher has an important contribution to make to assessment. The first eight points in the list of possible indicators of hearing loss given above may well not be observable outside the classroom. Specific observations of how a child handles communication in a variety of school situations is something which cannot be done by a teacher of the deaf who is not permanently in the child's classroom. The class teacher's role is important in full and ongoing assessment but that teacher may require guidance from a specialist upon the nature and relevance of observations. Webster and Ellwood (1985) outlined a profiling system that can be used by teachers in mainstream classes to help inform their educational practice with hearing-impaired children.

Strategies for classroom practice have been discussed widely in the literature on the education of hearing-impaired children and these are so complex that they require a full volume. Mainstream class teachers will generally have support and advice from specialist teachers of the deaf working either in a special unit in the school or visiting the school on a regular basis. Advice and guidance will be related to the language needs of children; to their experiential limitations and importantly, to the management of amplification systems. In some authorities specialist support teachers may be appointed to work with hearing-impaired children in mainstream classes. Such teachers may provide support in the classroom or extract the child for individual attention or may use a mixed approach. Whichever way the support is offered it is necessary for there to be a close working relationship between the mainstream teacher and the specialist. The mainstream teacher will be asked about planned work so that the specialist teacher can anticipate areas where preparatory work may be needed with the child. The specialist teacher may be asked to assist with work where the mainstream teacher has found that the child has had difficulties. In some instances specialist and mainstream teachers have adopted a team teaching approach to classroom management thus removing an overt focus of attention on the hearing-impaired child.

In some local authorities provision is made in mainstream schools for children who are being educated through some system of Sign or manual communication. It is unlikely that the mainstream class teacher will have sufficient skills in such communication modes to be able to provide all of the linguistic output for the child to access the curriculum let alone to promote language acquisition. These children obviously have a more severe level of special need and are usually placed in mainstream schools with a classroom support person – either a teacher or an assistant. It is important to consider the likely affect of the extra attention involved in the use of support staff. There is a danger that children will be denied making learning decisions for themselves. This high level of positive discrimination means that they are in danger of being exposed to excessive external control and this can be a major factor in the development of learned helplessness (Quigley and Kretschmer, 1982). Lynas (1986) researched the integration of hearing-impaired children into mainstream schools and reported the observations of both hearing and integrated hearing-impaired children about their feelings on excessive positive discrimination. Lynas saw this as being a factor which was likely to prejudice integration and was something which was deeply resented both by the hearing-impaired child and by hearing classmates. Intensive support in the mainstream class by especially employed helpers or by specialist teachers is a very good example of positive discrimination at its most excessive. The consequences for the developing child or young person could well be counter productive from both an integrational and an educational point of view.

There is a further aspect to this use of classroom support that we should be cautious about. In many cases the support is provided by someone described as an integration assistant. Such people may not be, and indeed very rarely are, qualified teachers – let alone specialist teachers of hearing-impaired children. They may be working under the guidance of a teacher of the deaf but may not receive supervision and monitoring. Such people will act as an interpreter or amanuensis particularly where the child has limited language skills and where the policy is for manual support. This practice raises several concerns. One is related to the functioning of this integration assistant. As has been pointed out, generally such people are not teachers and have little understanding of the principles of language acquisition or of how children generally think and learn. Observation of their work raises serious questions about the ability of such a system to facilitate language development. With adequate training this may be possible but the levels of knowledge and expertise observed by this writer would suggest that a great deal needs to be done.

REFERENCES

Andrews, E.M. (1988) 'The relationship between natural auralism and the maternal reflective way of working', *Journal of the British Association of Teachers of the Deaf*, 2, 5, 146–54.

BATOD (1989) 'Report on staffing and salary situation in schools', *Journal of the British Association of Teachers of the Deaf*, 2, 3, 2.

Department of Education and Science (1978) *Special Educational Needs* (The Warnock Report), London: HMSO.

Fraser, B.C. (1977) 'Integration', *Child: Care, Health and Development*, 3, 3, 201–12.

——(1990) 'The needs of hearing-impaired children and integration', in P. Evans and V. Varma, *Special Education: Past, Present and Future*, Lewes: Falmer Press.

Garner, M. (1985) 'The conductively deaf child – our problem', *Journal of the British Association of Teachers of the Deaf*, 9, 4, 95–100.

Lynas, W. (1986) *Integrating the Handicapped into Ordinary Schools: A study of hearing-impaired children*, London: Croom Helm.

Lynas, W., Huntington, A. and Tucker, I. (1988) *A Critical Examination of Different Approaches to Communication in the Education of Deaf Children*, The Ewing Foundation.

Newson, J. (1978) 'Dialogue and development', in A. Lock (ed.), *Action, Gesture and Symbol: The Emergence of Language*, London: Academic Press.

Quigley, S. and Kretschmer, R. (1982) *The Education of Deaf Children*, London: Edward Arnold.
Webster, A. and Ellwood, J. (1985) *The Hearing-Impaired Child in the Ordinary School*, London: Croom Helm.
Webster, A. and Wood, D. (1989) *Children With Hearing Difficulties*, London: Cassell.
Wood, D.J., Wood, H.A., Griffiths, A.J. and Howarth, C.I. (1986) *Teaching and Talking With Deaf Children*, London: John Wiley.

9

PHYSICAL DISABILITIES

Ian Glen

 Our perceptions of disability are often closely tied up with notions of mobility and access as typified by this sign now universally used to draw attention to public facilities for the disabled. The motif, depicting as it does a person in a wheelchair, serves as a generalisation for all the problems associated with physical disability, and while the use of symbolism in this way may be helpful in defining a group of people within the mainstream population, it also serves to mask the wide variety of individual difference which exists within that group. It is because the labels which we commonly use to describe different groups often shape our expectations of the potential of individual group members, that we need a broader knowledge of particular disabling conditions.

Earlier chapters of this book have already considered the problems of teaching children with difficulties, disorders and impairments, and this chapter in its turn is concerned with disabilities. These common terms, along with the global notion of handicap, are often used indiscriminately in education when discussing children who have special educational needs. However, such terms are not necessarily interchangeable, and an understanding of the concepts of impairment, disability and handicap are essential to teachers wishing to assess special educational need. Consider, for example, the situation of a teenage youngster who is confined to a wheelchair. One can certainly assume that there must be some degree of physical impairment preventing normal mobility. However, the child can only be considered disabled in respect of his or her inability to carry out the normal functions of daily living. For instance, he or she may be unable to walk or play games like football but may be perfectly able to perform on the recorder or violin and excel in the school orchestra. So is this particular child handicapped? That may depend, for example, on the layout of the school building. Should the school science laboratory be on the top floor and only accessible by means of a flight of stairs, then anyone in a wheelchair would be handicapped by this particular arrangement. Impairment can therefore be seen as a deficit which exists in the individual, for example as a result of a medical condition or an injury preventing normal functioning; disability can be described as the functional limitations of that individual as a result of the impairment; and handicap can be conceptualised in terms of the society and environment within which the person with an impairment has to function.

Children with physical impairments cannot be considered as a homogeneous group, and they may be expected to display the same diversity of characteristics and abilities as the normal population of which they are a part. However, although a child with a physical impairment may or may not have a resulting special educational need, an examination of common physical impairments and medical conditions will assist teachers in developing such children's abilities while avoiding unnecessarily handicapping them.

Traditionally, teachers have looked to the medical profession for an understanding of the reasons behind different categories of physical impairment. Ideas of physical impairment resulting either before, during or after birth, allow us to talk in terms of hereditary, congenital, traumatic and medical conditions. While this is important both for an understanding of an individual's prognosis, and for planning the support which may be necessary for the child and his or her family, it is not always so helpful in informing the teacher about appropriate educational provision – children with a similar medical diagnosis may still have little else in common. It can, however, be useful to think in terms of various degrees of motor disability arising from, for example, muscular or neuromuscular impairment, and of other functional disabilities resulting from a variety of medical conditions. In all cases, the major challenge for the teacher is to provide access for each child to a broad and balanced curriculum, whether by modifying the teaching environment, the curriculum itself, or both. There are thus several ways to classify physical impairments. They may be described either in terms of the parts of the body affected, by the particular clinical condition, or by the degree of severity of the impairment. In the first instance, for example, terms such as hemiplegia, paraplegia and quadriplegia, can be used to indicate impairments involving one side of the body, only the legs, or all four limbs, respectively.

There is also a wide range of clinical conditions which may give rise to motor deficit, and these include the following common muscular or neuromuscular impairments and skeletal defects:

Cerebral Palsy is a non-progressive disorder caused by damage to the brain either before or during birth, or in early childhood. There are three main types of cerebral palsy: spasticity, athetosis and ataxia, determined by the site of damage in the brain, each type characterised by a particular state of general muscle tone and associated patterns of movement, and sometimes also described by including the limbs involved. Spasticity results from damage to the motor cortex of the brain, and the increase in muscle tone leads to a poverty of movement. The limbs involved may be stiff, weak and difficult to move, and be subject to strong spasm or muscle contraction. Deep tendon reflexes are also increased in the affected limbs, and over a period imbalance between major muscle groups can also lead to some deformity of the limbs or trunk. By far the largest group of children with cerebral palsy, well over half, suffer from a degree of spasticity, although many children in this group may display the characteristics of more than just this type of cerebral palsy. Athetosis affects far fewer children with cerebral palsy, and is caused by damage to the basal ganglia, that part of the brain which organises the body's motor activity, and it is characterised by involuntary movements and a general lack of body control. The effect of this condition often results in facial grimacing, dribbling and difficulty with speaking, and serves to remind us that an accurate assessment of every child with a physical impairment is essential as most children in this particular group have no significant intellectual impairment. Ataxia is caused by damage to the cerebellum, and only affects about 5 per cent of children with cerebral palsy. As the cerebellum controls the body's equilibrium, children affected have problems with balance and muscle co-ordination characterised by difficulty with walking and negotiating their environment. Children affected appear clumsy and frequently fall. Whatever type of cerebral palsy most affects a child, and many may have a combination of types, the important consideration for the teacher is the degree of disability. Children with cerebral palsy embrace a wide range of competency in mobility and communication, although some are also quite likely to have additional problems associated with neurological damage such as epilepsy, impaired hearing or vision, or intellectual impairment.

Depending on the degree of motor impairment, children with cerebral palsy may walk unaided, need crutches or a wheelchair. The arrangement of the school and classrooms should facilitate movement, and close attention should be paid to providing furniture which assists the pupil's balance and posture – the advice of the physiotherapist or occupational therapist is invaluable in this respect. Many children with cerebral palsy may also have difficulties with fine motor control, particularly with regard to hand function. In handwriting, for example, children with low muscle tone may have a problem picking up, holding and loosening grip of a pencil, while children with spasticity may have insufficient control over its use. Any inconsistency in muscle tone will affect the precision of a child's handling of small objects, and activities such as writing, which also involve rotation of the wrist and fingers, pose particular problems. By definition, children with cerebral palsy have suffered a degree of brain damage, and although it is extremely important not to confuse any resulting motor impairment with intellectual impairment, it is common to find that the cognitive potential of such children may not always be realised. Many have difficulties with spatial awareness due to perceptual problems, and this may affect their ability to discriminate, match, copy or recognise pattern, all activities fundamental to cognitive development. The use of special equipment and the introduction of microtechnology into schools has allowed a much greater degree of independence for some children with motor impairments and perceptual difficulties. Systems now available in schools range from those that give control of a limited environment which may include page-turning, feeding and simple switching, through microcomputer systems which assist with communication and writing, to the more general use of computer programs for use by children with a wide range of learning difficulties. Over half of all children with cerebral palsy may be expected to have communication difficulties. In some cases this may be caused by a hearing impairment, but more generally such difficulties will result either from a limitation on the child's ability to understand or use language due to damage to the cerebral cortex, or to inadequate control over the speech organs. The teaching of such children with communication difficulties calls for a careful assessment by a speech therapist before a language programme can be instigated, and for younger children the programme may also deal with problems of eating and swallowing as well as vocalisation. A therapist may advise augmentative forms of communication, which involve signing or symbol systems such as Makaton and may use technological equipment of varying sophistication. Whatever the case, communication remains a two-way process, and is essential for each child's cognitive and social growth.

Muscular Dystrophy is characterised by a gradual and progressive weakening of the body as muscle cells are replaced by fat and fibrous tissue. The most common type (Duchenne) is inherited by boys through a gene carried by the mother, although it does occasionally occur with no evidence of family history. Early symptoms of the disease usually appear at the nursery stage, when the child is noticed to be clumsy or unstable, and this may have developed into an awkward gait by the time the child first attends school. The first effects of the disease are noticed as a weakness in the lower limbs, and throughout the primary school the child can be expected to find more and more difficulty in walking. By the time that the child transfers to secondary school he will probably need a wheelchair and in addition, some skeletal deformity will have become apparent. As the weakness progressively affects the upper trunk, fine-motor (manual) skills will deteriorate, although by using microtechnology the ability to write and to continue to participate in independent activity can usually be maintained. At some stage, however, due to the child's increasing dependence on others to meet his basic needs such as feeding and toileting, or to the unsuitability of the mainstream school premises for wheelchair use, he may be considered for transfer to a special school. As yet no effective treatment exists for this form of muscular dystrophy, and most children affected become aware that their condition is both progressive and terminal. Death usually occurs before the child leaves school, either from the heart becoming too weak, or from respiratory infection due to weakness of the lungs. Teachers need to be aware of the debilitating effect of the disease both in psychological as well as physical terms, and that as the child grows older he may require counselling to support him through each progressive loss of independence.

153

Skeletal Impairments include general conditions such as brittle bones and arthritis, specific conditions affecting certain parts of the body such as the spine, hips or feet, and the absence of one or more limbs. Most children with these conditions will attend mainstream schools, although those requiring surgery may spend some time in a hospital or special school in order to receive adequate medical and physiotherapy support while undergoing treatment.

Brittle bone disease (osteogenesis imperfecta) is caused by an abnormality of the protein collagen which is essential for building strong ligaments and bones, and children who have this condition are to a certain degree prone to fractures, often without apparent cause, depending on the severity of their condition. Frequent or severe fractures may lead to skeletal deformities, or require a child to resort to a mobility aid. As this condition is likely to restrict a child's participation in PE and games, the teacher should look for other opportunities for the child to be an active participant in class or team activities. Sensible arrangements should also be made for the child to avoid hazardous situations which may occur at playtime or during class changes, but they should ensure that the child's social development is not curtailed through over-protection.

Arthritis affects about one in a thousand children of school age, and juvenile rheumatoid arthritis, sometimes called Still's disease, peaks at the beginning and end of the primary stage, although only about one-third of these children will continue with the active disease into adulthood. The cause of Still's disease is uncertain, but it results in an enlargement of the spleen and lymph glands and inflames all the joints. Children experience periods of fever, pain and stiffness which may be relieved by drugs such as aspirin, and these are followed by periods of remission. This cycle may affect the child's growth or lead to skeletal deformity, and physiotherapy may be used to help prevent this. Such treatment is often intensive and painful, and children with this condition should not participate in activities which will strain or aggravate their joints. As with children who have brittle bone disease, however, opportunities should be found for participation in group and social activities.

A number of congenital orthopaedic conditions such as clubfoot (talipes) and dislocation of the hip, are relatively short-term problems in that they are normally corrected by surgery followed by physiotherapy often before the child reaches school age. Perthes' disease, an acquired dislocation of the hip, affects some children during their early school years, and although treatment will usually prevent physical disability, it may lead to a child being admitted to a special school for the duration of the therapy. Although the prognosis in such cases is good, the hospitalisation, possible change of school and restriction on movement for many months can be expected to have some effect on the child which may disturb normal behaviour patterns.

Curvature of the spine (scoliosis) is seldom attributable to any particular cause. It may be congenital, concomitant to a condition such as cerebral palsy, or more rarely nowadays result from infection. Scoliosis may often be corrected by surgery or alleviated by careful attention to a child's seating and posture. More traumatic in every sense, however, are the effects of spinal cord injuries, for example as a result of sporting injuries or road traffic accidents. Children subject to such a trauma have not only to come to terms with their disabilities, but to a completely new and constrained way of life. The degree of paralysis and loss of function which ensues is usually permanent, and is determined by the site of the major spinal lesions – the further up the spine, the greater the loss of bodily function – and is similar to many of the physical effects of spina bifida.

Many of the conditions already discussed may require the child to wear an orthopaedic splint or brace either during therapy, to aid mobility or for extra protection. The teacher must obviously find out why such aids are used and how they operate in order to assist the child when appropriate. Some children, however, may be fitted with an artificial limb (prosthesis), as a result of an amputation or because the child was born without one or more limbs. It is important to maintain a correct and comfortable fit to such an appliance, and to understand that in such cases the child is likely to come to regard the prosthesis more as a natural part of themselves than as an artificial aid.

Spina Bifida is a common term covering a group of related congenital conditions caused by a failure of the neural tube to develop completely and close during the early stages of pregnancy. As it is the neural tube which normally develops into the brain and spinal cord, these conditions can result in severe physical and intellectual impairment. In its mildest form, spina bifida occulta, although some of the spinal vertebrae have failed to cover the spinal cord (meninges) completely at some point, the cord itself is essentially normal and the defect is protected and covered by skin.

This condition rarely results in any significant physical impairment. More serious is the case in which the linings of the spinal cord bulge through a split in the vertebrae forming a meningocele – a sac containing cerebrospinal fluid – but with the spinal cord in its normal location. This sac may be removed surgically with little ill effect, but the condition can lead to minor physical impairment.

The most serious condition in this group, accounting for about three-quarters of the cases which result in significant physical impairment, is myelomeningocele. Again there is a protrusion from the spine, but in this case of the complete spinal cord itself on to the surface of the back. Early surgical closure of the defect will lessen the chance of infection but may not reduce the effect of the lesion in causing paralysis and loss of bodily function. Most children with this condition will also suffer from hydrocephalus resulting from a blockage of the circulation of cerebrospinal fluid in the brain often following the surgery to close the spinal lesion. Unless relieved by the insertion of a shunt or valve, the increase of pressure in the brain may lead to intellectual impairment, spastic paralysis in the lower limbs or epilepsy. Shunts for the relief of hydrocephalus, whether associated with spina bifida or otherwise, do occasionally become blocked or infected, and in any case will need replacing as the child grows.

As with children who have suffered traumatic spinal damage, the site of the lesions in spina bifida determine the degree of physical impairment. A child with a defect sited high on the spine will have normal function restricted to the upper trunk. There will therefore be considerable problems with mobility, bladder and bowel control. The lack of sensation in the lower body presents added problems. Soreness caused by ill-fitting appliances or continual incontinence may not be felt by the child, but could lead to ulceration and infection, and special care needs to be taken to check for pressure sores, burns, etc. Badly managed incontinence can have a damaging psychological effect on a child, and advice should be taken, and help given, to ensure that this is not the case. Children with spina bifida benefit from an upright posture to assist their circulation, digestion and kidney function; however, they may need callipers or braces and the assistance of crutches in order to stand upright and walk, depending on the extent of their muscle weakness and level of paralysis. Many will need a wheelchair for mobility. In all cases teachers may expect children to need time out for surgical intervention or physiotherapy at one or more stages of their development.

Although many children with spina bifida will fall within the normal range of intelligence, a significant number will be intellectually impaired. Learning difficulties as a result of visual and perceptual problems, limited attention span, underdeveloped spatial awareness, poor hand–eye co-ordination, and lack of fine motor control are common. Characteristically, the social and verbal skills of many children in this group mask underlying problems of comprehension and logical thought, and an informed and comprehensive assessment is essential for planning classroom programmes.

Motor impairment as a result of muscular or neuromuscular dysfunction has implications for the total development of the child. The ability to move around in and explore the environment, the ability to communicate with other people, the ability to join in social activity – these are all essentials to intellectual, emotional and social development. An accurate, multi-disciplinary assessment of the child's needs at all stages will help the teacher to determine potential and how to achieve it. However, a number of medical conditions, many of a chronic nature, may also result in a variety of disabilities, and the normal classroom teacher may be expected to accommodate them. Some are described below.

Asthma, allergies and associated respiratory conditions are commonplace in schools, and all teachers can expect to come across them during their careers. Asthma is a chronic condition which affects breathing, and it is best described as a shortness of breath and wheezing, often accompanied by a cough. The condition affects about 10 per cent of the school population and results from a narrowing of the bronchial tubes by a tightening of the muscles and by mucus secretion for a variety of reasons including over-exertion, stress and allergy to food, dust or pollen. There is a tendency for asthma to run in families, and although the causes are not yet fully understood, there is a likelihood that individuals are predisposed to the condition. Treatment is usually by drugs administered through an inhaler and may be taken as required to control an attack, or on a regular basis as a preventative measure. Teachers should become aware of factors which may trigger episodes in particular pupils, familiarise themselves with the child's medication requirements, and make sure that the child participates appropriately in any strenuous physical activities.

Other allergies which affect numbers of children include hay fever, eczema and rashes, chronic catarrh and migraine. Like asthma these generally occur through inhalation or ingestion of a particular trigger substance or through the emotional disturbance of a child already predisposed to the condition. Informed common sense should regulate such children's activity, and the teacher should be aware of any child needing regular medication.

Cystic Fibrosis is a hereditary condition affecting both boys and girls in which there is an abnormal secretion by the body's major glands, in particular mucus in the lungs and digestive system, and salt in the sweat glands. Although the condition is progressive and cannot yet be cured, with careful treatment and management more children are now surviving into adult life. The condition does not cause intellectual impairment, although as with muscular dystrophy, an affected child will become aware of the poor prognosis and will need support in coming to terms with its progression and eventual outcome.

Difficulties with breathing are usually associated with cystic fibrosis. The build-up of thick mucus in the bronchial tubes may produce wheezing, and regular physiotherapy with postural drainage to help clear the air passages is likely to be required and arrangements may need to be made in school for this to take place. Despite this regular treatment such children are prone to respiratory infection and will frequently need treatment with antibiotics; however, the resultant chronic cough is characteristic of the condition and should be dealt with in a positive way by encouraging the child to bring up phlegm rather than treating the condition as infectious.

Over-secretion in the digestive system may be treated by a high-protein diet and pancreatic gland extract. The child may also have an increased appetite in order to maintain an appropriate calorific intake and as a result need to pass stools more often. Arrangements may need to be made to accommodate the fact that the child's stools may also be very foul smelling due to the presence of undigested fats. The high content of salt in the sweat may pose a problem during strenuous activity or in hot weather, as excessive loss of salt may lead to acute illness. The teacher should monitor the level of the child's physical activity as a matter of course and be aware of any medication that has been prescribed.

Diabetes is another pancreatic condition, and results from a failure to produce sufficient quantities of the hormone insulin to control the amount of sugar in the blood. In childhood the condition is usually controlled by regular insulin injections and by a closely monitored diet. Low blood sugar levels may result in headaches, confusion, paleness and perspiration – when this happens additional sugar is required. High blood sugar levels may result in excessive thirst and frequent passing of urine, requiring insulin treatment. The teacher should become aware of the child's dietary and treatment requirements, and make sure that the recommended routine is adhered to.

Epilepsy is a generally used term covering convulsive disorders of the central nervous system. During an epileptic fit or convulsion, a child will experience a seizure or violent involuntary contraction of the muscles and may lose consciousness. Epilepsy occurs together with some of the conditions already discussed, such as hydrocephalus and particularly with some types of cerebral palsy. However, it can also occur as a result of an infection such as meningitis or after a head injury, but in most cases there is no apparent cause or symptom except the convulsion itself. There are several types of epilepsy, but the three major recognised forms are the grand mal, the petit mal and the focal fit. In the grand mal, or generalised fit, the child will often lose consciousness after crying out and falling down. The child's arms and legs may be stiffly extended at first and then go into a jerky spasm for a short time. Sometimes there will be a loss of continence, but the whole episode is unlikely to last for more than a minute or two. Afterwards the child is likely to be confused and tired. A focal fit has a similar pattern to the grand mal but only affects one part of the body, for example an arm, leg or one side of the face, although it may spread to the whole of one side of the body and consciousness may not be lost. The petit mal is a mild form of epilepsy which typically manifests as a staring spell or momentary lapse of attention. Other forms of petit mal present as brief spasms in certain muscle groups for example causing a particular limb to jerk, or drop attacks in which the child suddenly loses all muscle tone and consequently drops to the ground but recovers straight away.

Most children with epilepsy can lead a normal life under a suitable drug regime, and will be unlikely to have an episode in school, although it is as well to be aware that some children's epilepsy may be triggered by flickering light. However, extra care should be taken with laboratory and workshop activities, access to hazardous sports such as climbing and sailing should be carefully controlled, and swimming in particular should be on a one-to-one basis. Should a child have a fit, see that he or she is comfortable on the floor in a semi-prone position, protect from further injury by removing furniture if necessary, place a pillow or folded jacket under the head but do not put anything in the mouth. Check the breathing and pulse, and when the fit has finished ensure the child's breathing is unobstructed. If the fit has not ceased after a few minutes, send for medical assistance. Otherwise let the child sleep it off as appropriate.

Haemophilia is a hereditary condition affecting males but transmitted by females, in which the blood clots very slowly or not at all due to a deficiency in one of the body's clotting factors. Boys with haemophilia are therefore obviously at risk from external bleeding, for example as a result of injury. More importantly, however, they are also subject to internal bleeding into the tissues and joints, particularly around those areas in constant daily use such as the ankles, knees, hips, shoulders and elbows. Normal activities such as running or games may give rise to painful joints due to this slow internal bleeding, and eventually the deposits may affect the joint lining itself leading to a cycle of further bleeding with long-term effects on mobility. Clotting factor concentrates are now available to treat this condition, and a child will be encouraged to manage his haemophilia as soon as he is able, both in regulating his own behaviour in order to avoid physical stress or injury, and in seeking treatment when appropriate. Teachers should encourage this approach and assist the child to develop suitable recreational activities and realistic vocational ambitions.

Heart Conditions in children are far more likely to be congenital than acquired, and many such defects can be corrected by surgery during childhood. One in four children with Down's syndrome is also likely to have a heart condition. Rheumatic fever is another major cause of heart disease in young children. The physical development of children with a heart problem may be slower than normal and they may get breathless more easily than their peers and consequently show a blue tinge in their complexion. Moderate exercise should not be a problem, but such children should not engage in strenuous competitive activities. While a knowledge of a child's clinical condition is a necessary starting point, teachers are likely to find a knowledge of the degree of severity of a pupil's disability resulting from the impairment more informative.

COMMON EDUCATIONAL NEEDS

We have seen that children who have physical impairments do not form a homogeneous group, but we can, however, consider the many common educational needs resulting from their disabilities by using a classification based on whether they have a mildly, moderately or severely disabling condition.

Children with a mild physical impairment can by this definition be expected to be fairly mobile, to have the use of their arms, to be able to attend to their own bodily functions and to communicate effectively. They may, however, have some difficulty with fine-motor control, be clumsy or slower than other children.

Children with a moderate physical impairment can also generally be expected to get about by themselves either in a wheelchair or by using a walking aid, although they are more likely to need special facilities and assistance with toileting, and may also have difficulty with communication.

It is quite common for mainstream schools successfully to integrate pupils with mild or moderate physical impairments. Although this may require buildings having been suitably adapted and ancillary support provided, successful integration depends mainly on the quality of the classroom environment. Access to the curriculum must obviously take account of the layout and furniture of the class areas used, but special attention needs to be paid to individual postural requirements. This is most important, for example, where handwriting is concerned, when the sitting position needs to take into account general comfort and balance, as well as head, arm and hand control. Communication is also a key to learning and is essential for social interaction. Children with motor disorders may lack control over the muscles necessary for speech, their articulation may be poor and they may be difficult to understand. Such children's expressive language may not match their receptive abilities, but they may be assisted by the use of communication boards, typewriters or computer aids, either operating them directly, with adapted keyboards, by switch scanning or by pointer. Reference to a specialist communication aids centre will provide further information on assessment, and on a range of equipment such as book holders, page turners and audio/video systems to assist children with communication and to help minimise the problems caused by difficulties they may also have with fine-motor control.

Integration, however, implies more than just giving physical access to disabled pupils. It also requires the development of their independence in an environment which at the same time encourages positive attitudes towards disability from all children. This can only be achieved if teachers take into account both the importance of social and group influences when planning classroom activities, and also of their own expectations of successful learning taking place.

Children with severe physical impairments are currently most likely to be found in special schools. Such children are not usually able either to move around independently, manage their own bodily functions, or to communicate effectively, and most have severe learning difficulties. The intellectual potential of such severely disabled children, however, should never be under-estimated, as with specialist support and modern technological aids, their development may also often be significantly enhanced. A great many children with mild or moderate physical disabilities are currently educated in special schools or units where the basic educational programme concentrates on the improvement of motor control, on developing communication skills, and promoting emotional and social development. The introduction of the National Curriculum has served as a stimulus for the development of a broader base to the special school curriculum. The recent establishment of Conductive Education in Great Britain has also helped teachers focus on the proposition that children with motor disorders originating in the central nervous system can learn new ways to control their movement and become independent. This system, originally developed by Professor András Pető in Hungary, has as its goal orthofunction, that is for the child to have sufficient mastery of the motor disorder to be able to function in the community without the use of aids and not merely to cope with disability. In the continuing debate on the issue of integrating children with special needs into mainstream schools, we should remember that our main aim is the education of the child and that while integration may be a preferred means towards achieving our aim it is not an end in itself. A study by Howarth (1987) examined the effect of integrating children with physical disabilities on the practice of nine primary schools in four Local Education Authorities. It found that the integration of children with mild, moderate and severe physical impairment into mainstream primary schools was quite feasible, but concluded that two major factors were necessary prerequisites for it to be effective. First, sufficient support had to be made available to mainstream schools in terms of resources, professional expertise and in-service training, to allow the development of school policies which could accommodate the whole range of special need, and to assist teachers in coping with individual pupils' disabilities. Second, these policies had to allow sufficient access to the school's physical, social and educational programme – that is the whole curriculum – so that children with physical impairments could participate on equal terms with their peers.

For children with physical impairments, whether in mainstream or special schools, the same principle must apply – they should be encouraged to function in as normal a way as possible and to the best of their ability.

REFERENCES

Bleck, E.E. and Nagel, D.A. (1975) *Physically Handicapped Children – A Medical Atlas for Teachers*, New York: Grune and Stratton.

Booth, T. and Swann, W. (eds) (1987) *Including Pupils with Disabilities (Curricula For All)*, Milton Keynes: Open University Press.

Denier, P.L. (1983) *Resources for Teaching Young Children with Special Needs*, New York: Harcourt Brace Jovanovich.

Halliday, P. (1989) *Children with Physical Disabilities (Special Needs in Ordinary Schools)*, London: Cassell Educational.

Hegarty, S. and Pocklington, K. (1981) *Educating Pupils with Special Needs in the Ordinary School*, Windsor: NFER-Nelson.

——(1982) *Integration in Action*, Windsor: NFER-Nelson.

Howarth, S.B. (1987) *Effective Integration – Physically Handicapped Children in Primary Schools*, Windsor: NFER-Nelson.

Russell, P. (1989) *The Wheelchair Child*, London: Souvenir Press.

Widlake, P. (ed.) (1989) *Meeting Special Needs Within the Mainstream School (Special Children Handbook)*, London: Hutchinson Education and Special Children.

Williams, P. (ed.) (1988) *A Glossary of Special Education*, Milton Keynes: Open University Press.

Further reading

(*1991–2*) *Disability Rights Handbook*, London: Disability Alliance ERA.

10

PSYCHOLOGICAL AND HEALTH-RELATED PROBLEMS

Neil Hall

INTRODUCTION

Teachers have to deal with a vast array of psychological processes which are induced by children's ill-health and injury. When chronic diseases, physical disability and trauma occur in childhood and adolescence, very strong emotional responses are experienced. Children, like adults, may well be unaware of, deny or minimise the effects of their situation and fail to implement appropriate health care regimes. All children, especially those identified as having special needs, will vary enormously in their understanding of health problems and injury and the impact these may have upon their educational, personal and social development. This chapter considers certain psychological factors relevant for teachers and others concerned with meeting the special educational needs of children who have associated, or possibly causally related, health problems. To provide a context for this analysis there is an emphasis upon the psychological health of children who have been abused (physically, sexually, emotionally and/or by neglect) and those who have been diagnosed as being infected by HIV (Human Immuno-deficiency Virus) or those who have developed AIDS (Acquired Immune Deficiency Syndrome).

THE ROLE OF THE FAMILY

Teachers have a particularly important task in facilitating the responses of the child's family or caregivers. They will need to be aware of how ill-health can act as a stressor on all members of the child's family. Given that some families are distinctly more vulnerable than others, certain parents and siblings will require counselling and practical support (Frude, 1991). Of significance is the school's role in helping to relay information to parents on a regular basis about the educational and psychological progress of their child. This can help to prevent unnecessary fears and anxieties and, in some instances, when pressures are great, the development of unintentionally neglectful parenting. Careful monitoring of the impact that this information-giving role has can significantly help to pre-empt inappropriate responses being maintained at home both by the children and other members of the family.

It can be extremely difficult for people to empathise with the feelings of children who are striving to comprehend the personal significance of their health-related problems. There will be great variation in children's abilities to undertake this task and then to communicate this to significant others. Teachers can be fundamentally helpful to their pupils, as they struggle to gain a greater understanding of themselves within this specific area of their lives, by keeping to the forefront the many differing variables which can impact upon children with any health problem. Of major importance is the value which is ascribed to them as individuals within their own families, how they are viewed as somebody with significance in spite of and because of their health problem. Many chronically ill, disabled, abused and injured children report feeling that they are an enormous burden to their families. They wish they could pretend that their ill-health and/or abuse did not exist and that they could administer their medicines and health-care routines, or undertake therapy, in a way which did not attract any negative attention. Children who have been abused frequently express their regrets about the actions which follow disclosure.

There are some children who are determined enough to make use of a particular aspect of their health problem to exert some control over their family situation sufficient, in their view, to gain acknowledgement for the stress they are experiencing. This can inevitably develop very complex family dynamics in which the child's psychological and health needs become inextricably bound up with other family matters. There are also family situations in which a parent or a sibling seeks to use a child's ill-health as a means of perpetuating some particular complaint of their own, usually having some connection with a relationship difficulty in which undue regard is being given to somebody else's particular needs.

STRESS

Stress in children is experienced in many different areas of their lives, to differing degrees of intensity, for varying lengths of time, and with changing consequences. Within schools, teachers require a suitable basis for understanding the nature of stress–health relationships to enable them to construct appropriate learning and emotional environments. Teachers require the means for assessing the strengths of those relationships to enable them to intervene and, where possible, to offset any risk of stress-induced illness in their pupils. Teachers will also wish to be aware of how their own practices and school policies could increase the stress for any of their pupils (see, for example Elias, 1989).

There are many definitions of stress but of particular use to teachers is the one provided by Sarafino (1990), which states that stress is 'the condition that results when *person/environment* transactions lead the individual to perceive a *discrepancy*– whether real or not – between the *demands* of a situation and the *resources* of the person's biological, psychological, or social systems'. Each one of these four, inter-related components can be applied by teachers when considering whether or not a pupil is stressed. Essentially, this requires teachers to assess various observable behaviours, such as physiological responses (e.g. breathing rate, sighing or gasping), psychological responses (e.g. memory loss or distortion, facial expressions as indicators of specific emotions) and social responses (e.g. aggression, or non-compliance); and the specific demands of a particular task or event, such as the cognitive demands (e.g. of a scientific problem), the emotional demands (e.g. of being threatened by older children), the physical demands (e.g. of exercise for children who are ill) and the social demands (e.g. of being required to participate in a group activity). A useful way of looking at this would be along a continuum where, at one end, there is misperception and at the other end an accurate appraisal. That a child may perceive a discrepancy between their personal resources (biological, psychological, social) and the specific demands of a situation (cognitive, emotional, physical, social) can be at any point on the continuum. The stress that a child presents will always be of his or her construction. The teacher's task is to make an appropriate assessment to judge whether, and how, it will benefit the child to intervene.

How teachers communicate with parents and pupils about stress management can have a significant effect upon the well-being of children. In this context, Madders (1987) has produced a particularly useful resource. She considers how teachers and parents can instruct children, aged 5–18 years old, to practise both physical and psychological techniques of stress management. There are good examples of how to encourage children and adolescents to work in pairs. Relaxation tapes for both younger and older children have also been produced. There is much to be learnt from such a text. Teachers might well wish to consider making relaxation tapes of their own for particular pupils or specific situations. Personalised tapes have been particularly helpful for children who have manifested specific features of stress arising from having been sexually abused. These have successfully been incorporated into classroom interventions.

SELF-INJURY AND STEREOTYPICAL BEHAVIOUR

Certain groups of children with special educational needs, particularly those with visual impairments and severe learning difficulties (including autism), frequently display familiar patterns of self-injurious and stereotypical behaviour. Their rhythmical, highly repetitive, behaviours (often variously including hair-pulling, head-banging, self-slapping, eye-gouging, and/or biting different parts of their body) are both frightening and highly harmful, and often create considerable stress in the home and school situation. Children who have been abused are also known to involve themselves in a higher incidence of such behaviour. A major concern for teaching staff is determining the severity of such behaviour. This will include being clear about the possibility of life-threatening or permanently disabling episodes. Matson (1989) has succinctly reviewed such behaviour and notes that while boys are more likely than girls to present these problems there is no qualitative difference in the range or severity of the behaviours observed for either sex. Although children of all ages can present these alarming behaviours more has been written about those aged 10 or younger.

Another, alarming, example of deliberate self-harm is that of anorexia nervosa which, according to Werry (1979), is 'the only ready example of what seems to be a genuine psychosomatic disease'. The major characteristics of this condition are the intense fear of becoming fat, even though there is measurable weight loss, and a persistent, often deceitful, refusal to maintain body weight in relation to what is classed as minimal normal weight. Those who have this disorder, and it is mostly females, can present as if eating an appropriate amount of food but they will actually be utilising many devious means to avoid eating and/or getting rid of food, once it is ingested, by using purgatives or laxatives. Teachers will always need to work in conjunction with medical staff and/or psychologists when contributing to the care of a child with anorexia nervosa.

SEXUALISED BEHAVIOUR

Sexualised behaviour in children and adolescents can signify a range of personal difficulties, psychosexual problems and developmental needs. However, there have been many disagreements as to what is, or can be considered as, sexual about children's behaviour (Jackson, 1982). This has created both worry and difficulty for professionals and parents. For teachers, children's sexualised behaviour in school, in its widest definition, is a frequently occurring and often perfectly harmless activity. Sometimes, though, certain behaviours cannot be interpreted innocently.

Children with special educational needs, for many reasons which appear to be unidentified, are likely to exhibit a greater incidence of sexualised behaviours than other children. Mitchell (1987), in recognising this problem, discusses ways of changing the inappropriate sexual behaviour of both young people and adults with learning difficulties. Many of these behaviours will have their origins in a higher frequency of sexually abusive assaults than would be found in the school-age population in general. Others will arise as a consequence of inadequate sex education.

Reports obtained from a wide range of home, school and community settings describe children and adolescents being involved in self, and mutual, masturbation; attempted, and actual, intercourse (vaginal and anal), heterosexually and homosexually; sexually aggressive attacks; coprolalic behaviour (repetitively uttering strings of expletives); disinhibited exposure of genitalia; and acts of oral sex. It is the nature and range of these sexual behaviours, as frequently occurring aspects of some children's behaviour, which teachers need to consider. Little, however, is known about developmental aspects of the range of children's sexual behaviour, especially those children with special educational needs. Roberts (1980) explores the influence of television programmes, school and public environments, the family, peers, and religion on children's sexual behaviour. In her preface Roberts argues soundly that the aforementioned 'can only be adequately understood within the larger context of cultural values, social policies, and institutional traditions and practices'. Teachers need to assimilate these influences into a comprehensive understanding of children's behaviour and development by a rigorous self-examination of personal feelings and experiences.

Teachers are mostly obliged to comprehend this area of child psychology and development from their own intuitive understanding and probably their personal experience. However, four main sources of information exist to which teachers and others can usefully refer:

1 Interview studies;
2 Observational studies;
3 Theoretical analyses; and
4 Autobiographical accounts.

Interview studies have been undertaken both with children of all ages and across different national groups. The most authoritative of these is the highly illuminating, and often very funny, account provided by Goldman and Goldman (1989). From their structured interviews with children aged from 5 to 16, in Britain, North America, Scandinavia and Europe, information can be obtained about what children know of the different aspects of sexual activity, how babies are made, and differences in the physical development of girls and boys. Observational studies, based on data collected about children's physical development and sexual behaviour, detail the presence of genital play and masturbation in very young children. From this literature it is evident that young children develop a sexual identity from their earliest years. From other observational work, detailed descriptions have been collected of a range of young children's interactions with one another. In Calam and Franchi's (1987) research, parents who had abused, or were at risk of abusing, their young children were asked about bath-time and bedtime routines. Valuable and revealing information about adult–child sexualised interactions was gained. Teachers could amass considerable data on children's sexualised behaviour which could help them in their attempts to comprehend more fully this aspect of human development. Craig *et al.* (forthcoming) have produced an observation schedule for use in nursery and infant school settings, which enables teachers and nursery workers to record discrete interactions and self-enacted behaviours which often contribute to an overall pattern of sexualised behaviour. This schedule would appear to be particularly useful for collecting observational data about individual children with special needs.

There are also theoretical accounts, chiefly emanating from the writings of Freud (1977), but other examples have also been developed within the context of family dynamics (Mrazek and Mrazek, 1987). Retrospective accounts, mostly from women who were sexually abused by their fathers, detail the pain and repressed memories of horrific and seemingly endless assaults (Fraser, 1987). Rouf (1989) produced an inspiring example of how, as a child, she attempted to make sense of being abused by her father. In conjunction with a psychologist she has produced an excellent set of materials for schools (Peak and Rouf, 1987). What has yet to be undertaken, and this is clearly a major oversight, is the systematic collation of different children's accounts from child abuse investigations.

PAIN

Karoly *et al.* (1982) state that pain is 'medicine's most basic and pervasive symptom and yet children's pain remains generally unexplored in comparison with adults'. Many children's health problems involve a variety of painful experiences. These include pain that is related to surgery, chronic illness, different forms of physical and psychological treatment, and the taking of various medications. Studies of the pain children experience when being abused are still awaited. For some children the experience of pain will have no apparent physical basis and will be entirely related to psychological factors. There is little doubt that the experience of pain is a widely varying and subjective one. What is less recognised is that adults often underestimate the intensity of children's pain.

Eiser (1990), in an excellently written discussion on the psychological effects of chronic disease on children and their families, considers how children experience and understand pain; how pain in children can be measured, assessed and treated; and what relationships there may be between pain and changes in developmental levels. Teachers can have a major role in determining how children experience pain, primarily because of their skills in facilitating children's reporting of, and coping with, this phenomena. A range of media, educational tasks and therapeutic interventions have been used; the latter including relaxation exercises, puppet therapy, hypnosis and stress inoculation. All of these can help children and adolescents, in age-related ways, to appreciate the origins and development of their particular pain and, in appropriate circumstances, how this might affect their educational progress.

CHILD ABUSE

The identification of a child who has been abused, whether from self-disclosure, behavioural characteristics, confession by the perpetrator, or information from another source, always necessarily implicates a multi-disciplinary team in the assessment of that child's needs. Teachers often express fear about becoming involved in this process, sometimes because of the potential of having to work with the abusing parents, or of having to confront their own values and feelings about abused children, or even at the thought of providing evidence for a police investigation and possible attendance at various court proceedings.

The teacher's role in assessment is crucial because of the potential for supplying objective data about a child's behaviour over time. Psychologists will be able to focus upon a perspective of the child's personal interpretation of the events and consequences and will be able to consider the need, if any, for specific psychological interventions to deal with particular health-related problems. Where such consequences are likely to impinge upon a child's educational progress, psychologists will necessarily have to work in partnership with teachers, parents and the children.

If schools are to assess their own needs in relation to becoming effective in child protection work they will require the active participation of a multi-disciplinary group. It is essential that parents and pupils must also be considered as partners. Children who have been abused need to know that there are people who are willing to believe them and act on their behalf to protect, and then help, them. Abused children require frequently repeated, explicitly made, statements about their self-worth, their potential for change, and the ultimate possibility of being able to contain, manage and resolve the myriad of negative and destructive feelings which can at times overwhelm their thoughts and dislocate their lives.

CHILD ABUSE AND SPECIAL EDUCATIONAL NEEDS

Paradoxically, child abuse is insufficiently talked about in the context of special educational needs. However, there is growing evidence that children with special needs, as noted earlier in the discussion on sexualised behaviour, are far more vulnerable to being abused, in any of its forms (Ammerman *et al.*, 1991). Moreover, child abuse contributes more directly to children's special educational needs than has been hitherto acknowledged.

There seems to be a general unwillingness to comprehend the variety of ways in which children with special needs are powerless to protect themselves from the abuses of others. Children without language cannot readily communicate their distress; children with hearing impairments cannot easily use telephone helplines; children with physical disabilities may not have the means to escape from a perpetrator or defend themselves; children with visual impairments may never see their perpetrator or even know that he is there until an assault occurs; children with learning difficulties may never have the ability to communicate the abuse that they have encountered; and children with profound psychological disorders may come to occupy such a closed-off world that they may never feel able to disclose their abuse.

PHYSICAL ABUSE

From the medical perspective, the most commonly encountered physical abuses of children are 'soft-tissue injuries, burns, fractures, and head trauma' (Briggs, 1991). Teachers need to be aware of the distinguishing features of these abuses. Burns are found on all areas of children's bodies and, sadly, are known to have been caused by all types of, and methods of using, injuring instruments – soldering irons, matches, lighted cigarettes, electric fires, scalding hot water, chains. Bite marks are clearly non-accidental, the size of the bite helping to identify the age of the perpetrator. Bruises, like burns, can appear at any site on a child. Often distinguishing features, relating to the instrument used, are left on the body. These are as variable as the characteristic parallel, linear marks left when a child has been hit with the human hand or the frequently encountered patterning of small, circular burns from cigarettes. Other, more difficult to notice, physical abuses include deliberate and violent shaking and poisoning.

Where physical injury has been identified, or is suspected, key behavioural changes in children and parents can be significant indicators of whether or not the injury has been caused non-accidentally. This is especially evident in the high degree of alertness that is manifested by those children who are constantly in fear of being physically chastised. Teachers can come to recognise these children by noting a number of indicators, including the differences in parents' and children's accounts of how the injury was caused or why it should be sufficient for having been responsible for keeping the child away from school; failing to volunteer information about the nature of the child's injury; inappropriate levels of concern, either in gross exaggeration or failure to demonstrate, about their child's injury; general lack of emotional, sometimes physical, support to the injured child.

Helfer and Kempe (1980) provide a useful review of preventive measures which children and parents can use, at different stages in their lives, to help in dealing with many of the situations which are considered to be precursors to abuse.

EMOTIONAL ABUSE

Psychological and emotional abuse of children is the 'repeated pattern of behaviour that expresses to children that they are worthless, unwanted, unloved, or only of value in meeting another's needs' (Brassard *et al.*, 1991). Such behaviour, either by acts of commission or omission, consists of various distinct sub-types of maltreatment, as identified by the above authors: spurning (which combines rejection and hostile degradation); terrorising (the threat to cause harm); isolating (by deliberate intent); exploiting (often by engaging children in criminal acts of theft, pornography); denying emotional responsiveness (effectively avoiding any positive human interaction). Garbarino *et al.*, (1986) deal fully with these matters.

Emotionally abused children figure largely in the general population of children with special educational needs. These children have sometimes had a lifelong family experience of the denial of being valuable and thus will only be able to communicate near to zero expectations of their own abilities and potential. Besides learning difficulties, many emotional and behavioural problems are also considered to be correlated with the above forms of psychological abuse, including attempted suicide, anxiety disorders (e.g. school refusal, disturbed sleep patterns, social withdrawal), habit disorders and tics (e.g. jerking, nasal wheezing, facial grimaces, rapid eye blinking, ritualistic behaviour), and developmental delay.

NEGLECT

Green (1991) suggests that 'Neglect is often less obvious and less dramatic than physical or sexual abuse, and it is more difficult to measure and define'. Many aspects of neglect are unintentional and closely related to social and economic factors, such as poverty, unemployment, housing conditions, physical and mental health, family functioning and knowledge of child-care and control. Unlike other forms of child maltreatment, the identification of neglect is focused singularly upon the circumstances of the child's parents or caregivers. There is a long tradition of having standards of parenting or caregiving at the heart of any assessment of neglect (e.g. Bowlby, 1953).

According to Wolfe and Pierre (1989) some children 'fail to thrive' as a consequence of neglect and/or abuse. These children, who present significant growth delays, exhibit other developmental delays. Non-organic failure to thrive describes the child's arrested physical development resulting from the actions of significant others, primarily the child's parents. A diagnosis of organic failure to thrive confirms the presence of physical factors sufficient to account for the child's developmental and physical delay. Iwaniec *et al.* (1988) discuss the inter-relationships between emotional abuse, failure-to-thrive and parenting and is an excellent example of applying a problem-solving approach to apparently intractable parent–child difficulties.

Neglect, as Green (1991) contends, has a 'more severe impact on the child's cognitive and psychological functioning than physical or sexual abuse'. A teacher can often be critical in intervening with parents who present in a depressed state, or who seem preoccupied with matters which have no specific relevance to the day-to-day care of their child. Neglectful parents have often been identified by teachers because of inappropriate attention to their child's medical and physical needs.

Szur (1987) considers that emotionally abused children have 'more than ordinary difficulties in forming and maintaining relationships'. They have very poorly developed communication skills but, nonetheless, convey their profound sense of pain and distress through symbolic play and interactions. Szur suggests that neglected children develop 'distinctive and recurring personality patterns', which manifest themselves in: a lack of trust; anxiety about being suddenly dropped, 'unheld' or discarded; inappropriate and precocious sexualisation of relationships; having an inability to be satisfied by anything that anybody did for them; aggressive, violent behaviour; difficulties in learning and thought disorders. Teachers who have encountered such children will each have experienced the force of their pupils' 'humiliation, rage, despair and intensity of mental pain' (Szur, 1987).

SEXUAL ABUSE

Not all sexualized behaviour in children and adolescents will be indicative of sexual abuse. However, there are particular groups of sexualised behaviours which must be investigated. These include: those which are enacted aggressively; ones accompanied by overtly eroticised language; the acting out of adult sexual roles; and/or undisguised public masturbation.

Teachers should be aware of the course of children's sexual behaviour and development within the context of interactions and events within family life (Mrazek and Mrazek, 1987). People are still 'denying the existence, forms and prevalence of sexual abuse both inside and outside the family' (Hanks and Stratton, 1988). Numerous research reports and surveys (e.g. Walton, 1989; CSAU, 1988), continue to demonstrate that the majority of abusers are male (c. 90 per cent), and that most of these men (c. 65 per cent) are known to the children who are abused, either as their fathers (39 per cent), stepfathers (15 per cent) or mother's cohabitee (11 per cent).

There is a continuing debate about which children are most likely to be abused. Undoubtedly, girls and women are subject to more frequent sexual harassment, sexual assault and sexual violence than boys and men. Studies consistently show that girls are more likely than boys to disclose that they have been sexually abused. In the

Manchester study, 83 per cent of registered cases of sexual abuse were girls. The average age at registration was 10.2 years for girls and 9.2 years for boys (CSAU, 1988). Given that abuse is often being perpetrated for a considerable period before disclosure, sometimes for several years, the average ages at which children begin to be abused are likely to be considerably lower.

Boys may also under-report sexual abuse because of their sense of what it means to be masculine. One fear is that people will comment negatively upon their sexuality and consider them to be homosexual (Hunter, 1990). It can also be compounded by the general environment created in schools and in the media by a predominantly female focus in child abuse-prevention programmes. With recent scandals affecting residential schools for boys, particularly in the special education sector (Cross, 1990), perhaps there will be a greater concentration upon preventive programmes and intervention (O'Mahoney, 1989) and other facilities (such as the Boarding School telephone helpline developed in conjunction with Childline) for these children.

When children disclose abuse, irrespective of their ages or gender, they need to know explicitly that what they have said is valued by the teacher. These children are asking for something to be done to protect them from having to experience the abuse again. While a teacher cannot guarantee personal responsibility for protecting a child they must offer overtly to do everything they can (and this necessarily involves other people). Although many children request that what they have said should be kept secret their overwhelming need is for this information to be made public. Children are often asking for permission to make their disclosure general knowledge to those who can help. Teachers must not collude with children's feelings of negative self-worth and add to their perception of the power that the perpetrator already has over her or him. Sexually abused children consistently reflect on how they needed to share their hurt and sense of betrayal with people who would be able to offer support and validation for what they had been experiencing. In telling one person a child is symbolically telling everyone who is significant about their pain and distress.

Maher (1987) demonstrates the central role of teachers in the identification, and reporting, of abused children. The main message is simple, and is already adhered to in many circumstances within teaching: Every child has a right to be listened to carefully by teachers, in relation to what is being both implicitly and explicitly stated. Children's behaviour and development have to be observed carefully, recorded and reported when there is evidence of unanticipated or unusual changes. That this occurs ordinarily in classroom life is rarely disputed. However, when matters relate to the family, this does not always seem to have happened. Too frequently disclosures have not been reported because it was not thought possible that children could have been telling the truth about what their parents had done to them.

Sinason (1989) comments that the 'extra vulnerability of handicapped people to sexual abuse has only been properly acknowledged in the last few years'. All teachers, especially those of younger children and those with special needs should become acquainted with the general principles and practices of child abuse-prevention programmes. Elliott's work (1985; 1987) is pre-eminent in the United Kingdom (see also KIDSCAPE for primary-aged children, and TEENSCAPE for secondary children). Other useful resources (Milner and Blyth, 1989; Hillman and Solek-Tefft, 1988) are texts specifically written for teachers. Glaser and Frosh (1988) provide an authoritative account of child sexual abuse at both a theoretical and therapeutic level.

The most successful staff training programmes which deal with child sexual abuse, all include awareness-raising exercises about sexual experiences in childhood. Braun (1988) can be particularly recommended. Marsland and Farrell (1989) and Oldham CPTG (1988) also offer many useful activities for teachers and other school staff which can be undertaken individually or in groups.

HIV AND AIDS IN CHILDREN

Most children infected with HIV have had the virus transmitted from their mothers at birth or by receiving contaminated blood supplies, either during operations or from transfusions in relation to their haemophiliac condition. What remains unknown is the number of pupils in schools who are infected and undiagnosed because of intravenous drug use, sexual intercourse within relationships (heterosexual and homosexual), or from penetrative (vaginal or anal) sexual abuse. Many adults with AIDS have become infected with HIV while still adolescent and at school.

There is general agreement that HIV infection can only be

transmitted in three ways: sexual intercourse (vaginal and anal, and also from semen donation); blood (transfusions, used needles or syringes, organ and tissue transplants); from an infected mother to her child. Nonetheless, teachers and parents have justifiably expressed their concerns about the possibility of HIV infection at school. However, Mok (1989) states that 'No case of HIV infection has been transmitted in the school setting'. She advises that, unless there are special medical reasons for doing so, infected children at school should be treated the same as other children; they should have the same access to curricular activities as would other children with equivalent academic and physical abilities. This means the full range of indoor and outdoor lessons, including swimming and all contact sports. What will be necessary, however, is to help safeguard HIV-infected children from being in contact with other children who have any of the common childhood diseases, such as measles and chicken-pox.

The role of teachers in helping to normalise the lives of children with HIV infection or AIDS is crucial. This requires teachers to consider their own values about human behaviour. Notwithstanding prejudice and discrimination, this includes: the range of sexual behaviour and sexual preferences; issues relating to death, dying and bereavement; and intravenous drug use. Given that children with HIV or AIDS are attending school means that teachers need to be fully aware of the roles they can fulfil. Practical tasks can be undertaken in relation to the care of children with HIV or AIDS. As Peckham and Senturia (1987) state, 'School personnel should be trained in uniform procedures for handling blood and bodily secretions in schools to minimise transmission of HIV, hepatitis B, and other infectious agents'. The message is that good hygiene practices should be performed at all times for all children.

Teachers can also foster a better understanding of the nature of high-risk behaviours which can lead to children and young people becoming infected with HIV. In a discussion of the context and content of AIDS education, Dixon (1990) proposes a framework for considering both the needs of pupils and teachers. She argues for particular attention to be offered to children with special educational needs, given the many assumptions that people make about this school population: how they mature emotionally and form intimate relationships; how they are frequently unable to protect themselves from sexual exploitation and involvement in self-injurious activities, such as drug abuse; and how they often have limited opportunities for mixing in a range of social situations. For teachers who wish to adopt a more structured approach Beattie (1990) considers how, across subject boundaries and within the context of the National Curriculum, children's learning about personal and social health and development can be undertaken in relation to HIV and AIDS.

Adolescents have also taken initiatives in devising materials for AIDS education, as Hagedorn (1989) shows in her report of a play called *Gift-Wrapped*. Written by a group of 14-year-olds, from the London Borough of Haringey, the play was created by the pupils as a response to what they felt to be boring and useless AIDS videos and teaching materials. Dervish-Lang (1990) outlines the content of a game she has based on the British Medical Association's material *AIDS and You: An Illustrated Guide* (BMA, 1988). The game has been found to be particularly helpful for children with a range of special educational needs and also for those who have English as a second language.

Of relevance to such work is the research of Melton (1988) into the developmental aspects of adolescents' risk-taking behaviour as it relates to the perceived risks of developing AIDS. Neither younger nor older adolescents are likely to have any personal experience of someone of their peer group with AIDS. If this does occur then it will almost certainly arise as a consequence of that person having AIDS because of matters beyond their control, as with blood transfusions. Specific approaches must be targeted to those groups of adolescents who differ in the way they perceive and respond to the opportunity to take risks. As Melton (1988) argues, 'individuals who frequently engage in one form of risk-taking behaviour often have a lifestyle filled with potentially unsafe behaviour'. That this has been identified in some adolescents to include combining substance mis-use, including intravenous drug abuse, and frequent sexual activity with multiple partners, raises many questions about how safely any of these behaviours are being practised. Research information about the frequency of risky heterosexual and homosexual behaviour among adolescents is largely unknown. There is, as Frankham and Stronach (1990) suggest, a feeling of 'AIDS invulnerability' among many adolescents.

CONCLUSIONS

Applying a psychological perspective to understanding children's health-related problems can allow teachers to gain a more comprehensive insight into what may be contributing to their pupils' special educational needs. Overt behaviours, such as those which constitute self-injury, stereotypical reactions or eroticised interactions, can be either causally related to ill-health or associated with health-related problems. Psychological responses, such as those involved in children's experience of stress and pain, serve to indicate a range of difficulties which may have been encountered. An understanding of child abuse and HIV/AIDS is only possible by considering both the psychological and physical consequences of these phenomena.

REFERENCES

Ammerman, R.T., Lubetsky, M.J. and Drudy, K.F. (1991) 'Maltreatment of handicapped children', in R.T. Ammerman and M. Hersen (eds) *Children at Risk: An Evaluation of Factors Contributing to Child Abuse and Neglect*, New York: Plenum Press.

Beattie, A. (1990) 'Partners in prevention? AIDS, sex education and the National Curriculum', in D.R. Morgan (ed.) *AIDS: A Challenge in Education*, London: Institute of Biology.

Bowlby, J. (1953) *Child Care and the Growth of Love*, Harmondsworth: Penguin Books.

Brassard, M.R., Hart, S.N. and Hardy, D.B. (1991) 'Psychological and emotional abuse of children', in R.T. Ammerman and M. Hersen (eds) *Case Studies in Family Violence*, New York: Plenum Press.

Braun, D. (1988) *Responding to Child Abuse: Action and Planning for Teachers and Other Professionals*, London: Bedford Square Press.

Briggs, S.E. (1991) 'Medical issues with child victims of family violence', in R.T. Ammerman and M. Hersen (eds) *Case Studies in Family Violence*, New York: Plenum Press.

British Medical Association (1988) *AIDS and You: An Illustrated Guide*, London: British Medical Association.

Calam, R. and Franchi, C. (1987) *Child Abuse and its Consequences: Observational Approaches*, Cambridge: Cambridge University Press.

Child Sexual Abuse Unit (1988) 'Child sexual abuse in Greater Manchester: a regional profile', in C. Wattam, J. Hughes and H. Blagg (eds) (1989) *Child Sexual Abuse: Listening, Hearing and Validating the Experiences of Children*, Harlow: Longman.

Craft, A. (ed.) (1987) *Mental Handicap and Sexuality: Issues and Perspectives*, Tunbridge Wells: Costello.

Craig, O., Fairhurst, P., Hall, N., Lees, J. and Mason, I. (forthcoming)

Recording Concerns about Young Children's Sexual Behaviour: Developing an Observation Schedule.

Cross, J. (1990) 'Abuse of children in residential establishments', *SENNAC Discussion Paper*, Dept of Education, University of Liverpool.

Department of Health and Social Security (1986) *Working Together: A Guide to Arrangements for Inter-Agency Cooperation for the Protection of Children*, London: HMSO.

Dervish-Lang, L. (1990) 'Developing AIDS and HIV teaching materials for school children', in D.R. Morgan (ed.) *AIDS: A Challenge in Education*, London: Institute of Biology.

Dixon, H. (1990) 'Sensitivity to special needs in schools', in D.R. Morgan (ed.) *AIDS: A Challenge in Education*, London: Institute of Biology.

Eiser, C. (1990) *Chronic Childhood Disease: An Introduction to Psychological Theory and Research*, Cambridge: Cambridge University Press.

Elias, M.J. (1989) 'Schools as a source of stress to children: an analysis of causal and ameliorative influences', *Journal of School Psychology*, 27, 393–407.

Elliot, M. (1985) *Preventing Child Sexual Assault*, London: Bedford Square Press.

——(1987) *Keeping Safe: A Practical Guide to Talking with Children*, London: Bedford Square Press.

Frankham, J. and Stronach, I. (1990) *Making a Drama Out of a Crisis*, Norwich: University of East Anglia.

Fraser, S. (1987) *My Father's House*, London: Virago.

Freud, S. (1977) *On Sexuality: Three Essays on the Theory of Sexuality and Other Works*, Harmondsworth: Penguin Books.

Frude, N. (1991) *Understanding Family Problems: A Psychological Approach*, Chichester: Wiley.

Garbarino, J., Guttman, E. and Seeley, J.W. (1986) *The Psychologically Battered Child*, San Francisco: Jossey-Bass.

Glayser, D. and Frosh, S. (1988) *Child Sexual Abuse*, Basingstoke: Macmillan.

Goldman, R. and Goldman, J. (1986) *Show Me Yours: What Children Think About Sex*, Harmondsworth: Penguin.

Green, A. (1991) 'Child neglect', in R.T. Ammerman and M. Hersen, *Case Studies in Family Violence*, New York: Plenum Press.

Hagedorn, J. (1989) 'Drama out of crisis', *The Guardian*, 18th July, 1989.

Hanks, H. and Stratton, P. (1988) 'Family perspectives on early sexual abuse', in K. Browne, C. Davies and P. Stratton (eds) *Early Prediction and Prevention of Child Abuse*, Chichester: Wiley.

Health Education Authority (1990) *The Facts about HIV and AIDS: A Leaflet about HIV and AIDS and How to Protect Yourself*, London: Health Education Authority.

Helfer, R.E. and Kempe, C.H. (1980) 'An overview of prevention', in C.H. Kempe and R.E. Helfer (eds) *The Battered Child* (3rd edn), Chicago: University of Chicago Press.

Hillman, D. and Solek-Tefft, J. (1988) *Spiders and Flies: Help for Parents and Teachers of Sexually Abused Children*, Lexington, MA: Lexington Books.

Hunter, M. (1990) *Abused Boys: The Neglected Victims of Sexual Abuse*, Lexington, MA: Lexington Books.

Iwaniec, D., Hertbert, M. and Sluckin, A. (1988) 'Helping emotionally abuse children who fail to thrive', in K. Browne, C. Davies and P. Stratton (eds) *Early Prediction and Prevention of Child Abuse*, Chichester: Wiley.

Jackson, S. (1982) *Childhood and Sexuality*, Oxford: Blackwell.

Karoly, P., Steffen, J.J. and O'Grady, D.J. (eds) (1982) *Child Health Psychology: Concepts and Issues*, New York: Pergamon Press.

Madders, J. (1987) *Relax and be Happy: Techniques for 5–18 Year Olds*, London: Unwin.

Maher, P. (ed.) (1987) *Child Abuse: The Educational Perspective*, Oxford: Blackwell.

——(1987a) 'School responses to child abuse cases: the reactive role', in P. Maher (ed.) *Child Abuse: The Educational Perspective*, Oxford: Blackwell.

——(1987b) 'The school's proactive role in reducing levels of child abuse', in P. Maher (ed.) *Child Abuse: The Educational Perspective*, Oxford: Blackwell.

Marsland, P. and Farrell, P. (eds) (1989) *What's Different About This Child Today? Issues in Child Protection for Schools, Manchester*: NSPCC North Manchester/University of Manchester.

Matson, J. (1989) 'Self-injury and stereotypies', in T.H. Ollendick and M. Hersen (eds) *Handbook of Child Psychopathology*, 2nd edn, New York: Plenum Press.

Melton, G. (1988) 'Adolescents and prevention of AIDS', *Professional Psychology: Research and Practice*, 19, 4, 403–8.

Milner, J. and Blyth, E. (1989) *Coping With Child Sexual Abuse: A Guide For Teachers*, London: Longman.

Mitchell, L.K. (1987) 'Intervention in the inappropriate sexual behaviour of individuals with mental handicaps', in A. Craft (ed.) *Mental Handicap and Sexuality: Issues and Perspectives*, Tunbridge Wells: Costello.

Mok, J. (1989) 'Paediatric HIV infection', in J. Green and A. McCreaver (eds) *Counselling in HIV Infection and AIDS*, Oxford: Blackwell.

Mrazek, D.A. and Mrazek, P.B. (1987) 'Psychosexual development within the family', in P.B. Mrazek and C.H. Kempe (eds) *Sexually Abused Children and Their Families*, Oxford: Pergamon Press.

Oldham CPTG (1988) *Child Protection: Two 2-Day Courses for Teachers*, Oldham: Oldham Metropolitan Borough.

O'Mahoney, B. (1989) 'Key issues in managing adolescent sexual behaviour in residential establishments', in J. Christopherson *et al.* (eds) (1989) *Working with Sexually Abused Boys: An Introduction for Practitioners*, London: National Children's Bureau.

Peak, A. and Rouf, K. (1987) *Working with Abused Children: A Resource Pack for Professionals*, London: Children's Society.

Peckham, C. and Senturia, Y. (1987) 'Transmission of HIV infection: implications for fostering and adoption', in D. Batty (ed.) *The Implications of AIDS for Children in Care*, London: British Agencies for Adoption and Fostering.

Roberts, E.J. (ed.) (1980) *Childhood Sexual Learning: The Unwritten Curriculum*, Cambridge, MA: Ballinger.

Rouf, K. (1989) *Secrets*, London: The Children's Society.

Sarafino, E.P. (1990) *Health Psychology: Biopsychosocial Interactions*, New York: Wiley.

Sinason, V. (1989) 'Uncovering and responding to sexual abuse in psychotherapeutic settings', in H. Brown and A. Craft (eds) *Thinking the Unthinkable: Papers on Sexual Abuse and People with Learning Difficulties*, London: Family Planning Association Education Unit.

Szur, R. (1987) 'Emotional abuse and neglect', in P. Maher (ed.) *Child Abuse: The Educational Perspective*, Oxford: Blackwell.

Walton, M. (1989) 'What use are statistics? – policy and practice in child abuse', in C. Wattam, J. Hughes and H. Blagg (eds) *Child Sexual Abuse: Listening, Hearing and Validating the Experiences of Children*, Harlow: Longman.

Werry, J.S. (1979) 'Psychosomatic disorders, psychogenic symptoms, and hospitalization', in H.C. Quay and J.S. Werry (eds) *Psychopathological Disorders of Childhood* (2nd edn), New York: Wiley.

Wolfe, D.A. and Pierre, J.St. (1989) 'Child abuse and neglect', in T.H. Ollendick and M. Hersen (eds) *Handbook of Child Psychopathology*, New York: Plenum Press.

11

MULTI-SENSORY IMPAIRMENTS

Heather Murdoch

Anthony is eight years old. His hearing and vision are impaired. He rarely responds to 'everyday' sounds around him, but seems attracted to loud music; he does not respond to his name or to spoken language, although he may pause at a shout. He peers closely at objects, and often collides with people and obstacles in his path. He may move towards lights and large shiny objects, especially red ones. He has glasses, and usually wears them. Hearing aids have been prescribed, but Anthony rejects them; he also suffers from frequent ear infections.

Anthony is ambulant, but reluctantly so. He is more or less toilet-trained. He shows some understanding of cause and effect (enjoying pop-up toys, turning on taps to play with the water) and is working in school on various sorting and matching activities. He likes bouncing, swinging, fairground rides and most activities involving sensations of movement. He enjoys fizzy drinks and snacks.

Anthony has been taught basic signs, for 'sweet', 'drink' and 'please'. He will use the movements if physically prompted, but shows no awareness that the signs have different meanings. He knows the uses of many everyday objects; for instance, if an adult approaches with his cup, he expects a drink. He may manhandle adults to show that he wants something. Swinging, for example, is one of his favourite activities, and he may try to pull an adult out of the classroom and towards the swings. If his actions are disregarded, or not understood, he may become distressed or may simply wander off.

Anthony tends to accept whatever happens to him, and often shows scant response to changes in activity. Alterations in routine, however, may provoke responses which seem illogical to the adults around him. He may heartily eat a picnic lunch on an outing, yet repeatedly pull an adult towards the dining room on return to school. Sometimes he cries without apparent cause; sometimes he slaps his head. He will spend quite long periods fingering a Lego block, or a small carved wooden toy, intermittently watching his hands, and murmuring softly. He often seems in a world of his own.

DEVELOPMENTAL IMPLICATIONS OF MULTI-SENSORY IMPAIRMENT

Anthony is a child with multi-sensory impairment, or deaf-blindness. He is not 'typical', because no child with multi-sensory impairment is 'typical': variations in severity of hearing impairment, visual impairment and additional disabilities (if present) combine with the usual variations in aptitude, ability, personal and environmental factors to ensure uniqueness. Children with multi-sensory impairment may appear little affected, or may be profoundly dependent. The features of Anthony's behaviour mentioned above, however, serve to illustrate some implications of multi-sensory impairment.

Sight and hearing are the 'distance' senses. We see and hear people, places, objects and events over a considerable range and in considerable detail. Other senses do not share this role, offering detailed information only about the immediate, current environment. Many children with multi-sensory impairment, like Anthony, have some useful sight and/or hearing. The information provided, however, is incomplete, often distorted, deficient in quality and quantity. This has enormous implications for understanding and controlling the environment. It is distance-sensory information (from sight and hearing) that allows us to anticipate and act to influence events affecting us, and to monitor the effects of our own and others' actions. Touch, taste, smell and the movement and balance senses cannot effectively compensate for this role.

Some children with multi-sensory impairment, functioning in their early years as severely handicapped, appear to respond more readily to auditory and visual stimuli as they grow older. This process rarely reflects an improvement in their sight or hearing. A key factor is usually that of appropriate intervention, helping children learn to integrate and make optimal use of the limited sensory information they receive.

Anthony seems to gain enjoyment from both his sight and his hearing, since he moves towards sources of visual and auditory stimuli. The account suggests, however, that he shows more overt enjoyment of more immediate sensory experiences – movement, food and drink. He uses visual information to extend his knowledge of his environment (examining objects closely), but both sight and hearing are likely to present him with inconsistent, distorted signals which may cause confusion. He does not yet perceive benefit in his hearing being aided.

Our response to situations is based on a process of sensory integration. As described by Smith and Shane Cote (1982), this involves four stages. Initially, sensory stimuli are received through all available channels (for instance, olfactory and visual). The second stage involves perception: identification of the meaning of stimuli (the smell of toast burning, the sight of smoke pouring from the toaster). In the third stage, current information is compared to that stored in memory from past experiences, adding another layer to the interpretation (any moment now, the toast may catch fire). Finally an adaptive response to the situation is planned and executed (turn the toaster off as quickly as possible).

For the child with multi-sensory impairment, the first and/or second stages of this process are flawed. However good the child's performance on the later stages, the adaptive response produced will be based on inadequate, distorted, fragmentary information. No wonder that Anthony's actions may sometimes seem illogical to sighted hearing adults. Situations with little intrinsic meaning or motivation may trigger adaptive responses involving passive acceptance in preference to trying to predict or control; such attempts are unlikely to be successful, or worth the effort. Withdrawal to the restricted world of a small toy, or apparently groundless distress, may be responses to situations where too little information creates too much stress. Routines, on the other hand, provide experiences to which (through long practice) he knows the answers: he can produce appropriate responses which work well, like going to the dining room at lunch time. Changes to known routines, however, threaten Anthony's knowledge of how the world works. His response may be to try to maintain the routine, or at least the aspects of it which are available to him. Anthony's understanding of the school day may include having lunch, in the dining room, before certain other events (such as going home) happen. If lunch time passes while the class are out of school, it may seem appropriate to go to the dining room on return. Hunger or greed are not at issue; maintaining the routine is.

Multi-sensory impairment 'alters the way in which the individual 1) receives and sends information, and 2) interacts with the social and physical environment' (Siegel-Causey and Downing 1987, p. 20). This process begins at birth. Early attachment or bonding between carer and infant is a first stage in the child's development of social relationships, communication and cognitive concepts. The quality of attachment depends upon the quality of infant–carer interaction, with consistent, appropriate, predictable responses from the carer supporting secure attachment (Ainsworth *et al.*, 1978; Lamb, 1981). Infants with multi-sensory impairment may send obscure signals (stilling, an apparent lack of awareness, unexpected movements) which carers find hard to interpret. In turn, the child's information about the carer's responses may be too limited for consistency to be perceived (van Dijk, 1991). Children with multi-sensory impairment are particularly disadvantaged when moving away from the carer to explore the environment. They may be unable to hear or see the carer and thus maintain contact and security; in addition, if the carer moves away the child may be unable to find the carer again (Nafstad, 1989).

Difficulties at these early stages will affect further communicative and cognitive development. The child with multi-sensory impairment needs to 'discover his or her own body as an instrument with which to explore the world' (Writer, 1987, p. 191). Sight and hearing provide information about people, objects, events and the effects of the child's own actions, promoting movement, motivation and learning. The child with multi-sensory impairment needs appropriate intervention to be aware of, and interact with, the external world. This interaction forms the basis for global learning and development (van Dijk 1986, 1989).

Anthony appears to have mastered segments of the world around him – familiar objects, for example, and the concept of cause and effect. Cause and effect is involved also in his communication. Anthony, pulling at an adult, provides the cause from which he expects the effect of going to the swings. For this activity, at least, he has a means of controlling what happens to him. He does not, however, have a 'back-up' strategy if his first attempt at communication fails; neither does he yet understand the one symbol:one referent correspondence (one sign:one specific meaning) that he needs for formal symbolic communication. At present he is limited to communication about immediately available topics – he can take the adult to the swings, but only when the swings are nearby. His reactions to changes in activity, as noted above, suggest that his confidence and understanding are limited.

Independent movement increases the child's control of the environment, allowing a pro-active role in, for example, establishing that the formless space around the child has boundaries. The motor and mobility development of children with multi-sensory impairment, however, will be subject to the same constraints as that of children with visual impairments (see Chapter 7). The child with multi-sensory impairment, in addition, may be unable to use auditory clues, or to be encouraged by an adult's verbal support. The development of motor and mobility skills is closely linked to the child's security out of contact with the carer, and confidence in controlling the carer's proximity. Children with multi-sensory impairment and additional motor impairments have the same need to know that classrooms have walls, that doors open and shut, that physical movement (however slight) can affect the world around. The need to gain access to the environment is the same; the method of accessing may differ, with a greater emphasis on the adult bringing the environment to the child.

Children with multi-sensory impairment cannot use auditory information to compensate for the effects of visual disability, or visual information to offset their hearing impairments. Additional disabilities will further compound children's problems in gathering and using sensory information. If physical disabilities preclude exploration of the environment, there will be less sensory stimuli to perceive; learning difficulties will hinder the interpretation of information. Each disability interacts with every other. 'It is accepted that any deaf-blind child will have very great difficulties with learning but the cause of those difficulties may not be separable into problems of sensory perception on the one hand and information processing on the other' (DES, 1989, p. 4).

There is little information available on the global developmental patterns of children with multi-sensory impairment, and the uniqueness of each child's hearing impairment, visual impairment, abilities, disabilities and individuality seem to preclude useful generalisations. In the absence of evidence to the contrary, the usual assumption is that they follow the same course of development as sighted hearing children. This may not be the case: Fox (1983) argues that developmental milestones for children with multi-sensory impairment 'are irrelevant because their developmental route may be "cross-country", utilising different pathways and crossroads to their "normal" peers' (p. 67). Even if the patterns of development are those of sighted hearing children, the behaviours exhibited at particular stages are unlikely to be the same. Consider stacking blocks – the sighted hearing child sees the tower build up, and sees and hears it fall; each block is placed on the basis of visual judgement. Adults or other children may comment on the growing tower, and the stack is built in the context of the child's familiarity with piles of dishes, piles of laundry and other items. For the child with multi-sensory impairment, the activity is different: different components, different rewards, different skills, indicative of different abilities. To expect a child with multi-sensory impairment to stack blocks (or want to do so) because his sighted hearing peer would enjoy the game is to fail to understand the implications of multi-sensory impairment.

THE NATURE OF MULTI-SENSORY IMPAIRMENT

The discussion above may suggest, rightly, that multi-sensory impairment is not easy to define. Early definitions stressed degrees of auditory and visual impairment, but this approach did not consider the cumulative, interactive effects of the disabilities. Recent attempts at definition have included the following factors:

1 Multi-sensory impairment is not an additive combination of visual impairment and hearing impairment. 'The deaf-blind child is not a deaf child who cannot see or a blind child who cannot hear' (McInnes and Treffry, 1982, p. 2). Both distance senses are impaired, uniquely affecting the information the individual receives from the environment.

2 Children with multi-sensory impairment may have useful residual hearing and vision. A 1986 UK survey considered four

categories of disability: blindness with profound deafness, partial sight with profound deafness, blindness with partial hearing and partial sight with partial hearing. The last category held the largest number of children (DES, 1989). The combination of distance sensory impairments is a more relevant factor than totality of impairment.

3 Many children with multi-sensory impairment have further disabilities (for example, learning difficulties or motor impairments).

4 Educational provision for children with hearing impairment, visual impairment or learning difficulties may not appropriately meet the complex needs of children with multi-sensory impairment.

The range of needs presented by children with multi-sensory impairment is very wide; the prevalence of the disability is very low. The 1986 survey suggested the prevalence of multi-sensory impairment among the UK school population to be around one in 10,000 (DES, 1989), although more recent estimates have proposed one in 5,000 (Hills, 1991).

Congenital multi-sensory impairment may be caused by maternal viral infection during pregnancy (for example rubella, cytomegalovirus), prematurity and associated medical needs, birth trauma (for example anoxia) or genetic syndromes. Multi-sensory impairment not present at birth but manifesting during school age may be due to injury, illness (meningitis for example) or genetic disorders (for example Usher's syndrome, causing congenital deafness with subsequent visual loss).

Until recently, maternal rubella infection was the major single cause of congenital multi-sensory impairment in developed countries. Vaccination programmes, and new medical techniques for maintaining very frail babies, are changing the pattern of causation. Fewer babies with congenital rubella are being born; fewer babies with profound and multiple disabilities are dying.

Changing patterns of causation are reflected in changing patterns of need among the population, and changing perceptions among educators. Auditory and visual impairments may involve damage to the ears and eyes, and/or to the brain. In the past, children with cortical impairments were less likely to be assessed as having multi-sensory impairment. The sensory needs of children at very early developmental levels (whose auditory and visual systems function as those of very young babies) are increasingly being recognised.

Children with multi-sensory impairment are prone to additional disabilities; in the UK, one survey found a prevalence of 69 per cent (Best, 1983). Another found that most children with deaf-blindness had at least one additional disability, with nearly two-thirds perceived as having severe learning difficulties (DES, 1989). (The problems inherent in accurate assessment of children with multi-sensory impairment are discussed below.) A high incidence of additional disabilities is unsurprising: an insult sufficient to damage a baby's visual and auditory systems is likely to be capable of damaging other systems as well.

RESOURCES AND PROVISION

Multi-sensory impairment creates a complexity of need, demanding a multi-disciplinary approach to assessment and intervention. The low incidence of the disability, however, handicaps the development of expertise among educational, medical, paramedical and social services professionals. In this context, specialist training and organisations focusing on needs relating to multi-sensory impairment have great importance.

In the UK, SENSE (The National Deaf-Blind and Rubella Association) was founded in the 1950s by parents of rubella-handicapped children. It is now a national voluntary organisation, offering direct services (particularly to the pre- and post-school age groups) and operating as a campaigning and enabling body, offering support to families, service providers and legislators, and working to develop further services. Other voluntary organisations which focus on the needs of the multi-sensory impaired population include the National Deaf-Blind League, the Royal National Institute for the Blind and the Royal National Institute for the Deaf.

The International Association for the Education of the Deaf-Blind (IAEDB) encourages the exchange of information, teaching approaches and research world-wide. Again, the very low incidence of multi-sensory impairment, and the wide range of associated needs, create a need for this process; expertise initially developed in particular schools or units now forms part of the range of approaches from which educators in many countries can develop programmes for individual children.

In the UK, educational provision for children with multi-sensory impairment is currently in a state of flux. At present children are rarely integrated into mainstream provision, but are often educated alongside children with other disabilities. Two factors affect provision: the low incidence of multi-sensory impairment, and the very wide range of associated needs.

Specialist units for children with multi-sensory impairment have historically been attached to schools for children with hearing impairment, visual impairment or learning difficulties, and the majority have offered residential provision outside the maintained sector. These units have educated a minority of the multi-sensory impaired population, with most children educated in local schools for children with severe learning difficulties or physical handicaps, and some attending provision for children with hearing or visual impairments.

The geographical distribution of the units has in effect created regional specialist provision, although there have been no clear boundaries and some areas have no unit. The 1989 DES policy statement, *Educational Provision for Deaf-Blind Children*, suggested the further development of regional provision, and offered a model which might support the full ranges of age and need. Local authorities are now establishing peripatetic support services to maintain appropriate local provision within a region.

As noted above, the low incidence of multi-sensory impairment means that local provision often entails integration with children with other disabilities. The needs of teachers working with these children are in turn affected by factors related to the low incidence. Expertise is not readily available; non-specialist teachers may not have met children with similar needs, and specialist teachers are in danger of being isolated in their field. Class teachers need information relating to the use and development of residual vision and hearing, creating an appropriate learning environment and appropriate intervention strategies relating to communication and curricular access. They may need support in providing appropriate staffing ratios (often one-to-one for communication and other learning).

Teacher training programmes relating specifically to multi-sensory impairment are rare. In the UK, subject to certain mitigations, a teacher 'of a class of pupils who are both hearing impaired and visually impaired' is required by the DES to possess 'a qualification approved by the Secretary of State' (Great Britain, 1989, para. 17). Currently the only DES-recognised qualification involves a one-year full-time course offered by the University of Birmingham to experienced teachers of children with special educational needs. Short courses help develop expertise among teachers, educational assistants and other professionals, and are offered by a range of organisations including SENSE and the RNIB. Videos, journal articles and books are also increasingly available.

ASSESSMENT AND INTERVENTION: PRINCIPLES AND PRACTICES

Appropriate provision and intervention depend upon accurate assessment of needs. Impaired vision and hearing slow the pace of learning, because so little information is available to children about their environment and the effects of their actions. Assessment involving comparison with sighted hearing children therefore tends to indicate that children with multi-sensory impairment have severe learning difficulties. It is not always as straightforward to differentiate difficulties related to reception of sensory information from those related to cognitive processing of information received. Comparison with sighted hearing children is inappropriate for children with multi-sensory impairment.

Assessment materials designed for use with children with multi-sensory impairment are rare, and require sensitive use in the context of individual variations in hearing impairment, visual impairment, appropriate intervention to date and additional (for example motor) disabilities. Assessment of current functioning involves the need to analyse activities in terms of the information available to the child with multi-sensory impairment; this process is mentioned above. Assessment of potential demands even greater expertise and empathy, and prognoses issued by those unfamiliar with multi-sensory impairment should be interpreted with a great deal of caution.

Multi-disciplinary assessment should enable the child to be approached as an individual, rather than as a set of eyes, ears and problems. Assessment of separate faculties in turn may lead to conflicting advice – for example, physiotherapy recommendations on side-lying may leave the child's 'better ear' facing the mat rather than the outside world. Many children with multi-sensory impairment show apparently inconsistent responses. Hunger, fatigue, illness, medication, discomfort, environmental distractions, physical position, the demands of other disabilities or sensory overload may affect children's use of residual vision and hearing, and overall performance. 'Assessments of multiply handicapped children should depend on observational techniques and should take place over a period of time in the environment in which the child is spending the majority of his waking hours' (Wyman, 1986, p. 89).

Those assessing need to know about multi-sensory impairment, and about the child. A sudden approach by an unfamiliar adult, for example, may appear to the child as aggression and provoke a response in kind, which may in turn be misinterpreted. An appropriate base-line is the child's current performance, analysed in detail in the context of the information available to the child. Using developmentally based scales to indicate what the child is not doing is a less appropriate basis for intervention.

One framework for developing an educational approach for assessment and intervention involves viewing children's behaviours as adaptive responses to their perceived environment. This approach emphasises two aspects:

1 It attaches meaning to the child's behaviours, precluding responses such as 'she always twirls around', 'he slaps his head for no reason' and 'she won't walk on her own because she's deaf-blind'. Although the reason for the child's behaviour may not be apparent, the onus of interpretation is placed upon the adult rather than the child.
2 It stresses the importance of the child's surroundings (including places, people, objects and events).

Children with multi-sensory impairment receive imperfect, distorted, fragmented information about their surroundings. If they are to make optimal use of this information, the environment must be presented as clearly as possible. Educational approaches incorporating the following factors support children's attempts to make sense of their environment.

Establishing attachment between the child and the adult
Restricting the number of adults involved with the child is an obvious first step. 'In the education of deaf-blind children, development of responsivity is only possible when enough hours

can be spent with the child individually and undisturbed' (Visser, 1988, p. 5). Coactive movement, with the child and adult moving together in close physical proximity, allows the child to become aware of the adult, and allows the adult to notice and respond to small signals from the child. Sensitivity and responsivity to the child's signals mirror the process of attachment for sighted hearing children. Object and motor signals can help the child establish the adult's identity – for example, a distinctive bracelet to which the adult draws the child's attention at each meeting; a favourite jumping game with which adult and child begin each session (van Dijk, 1986).

Offering consistency of environment and approach A physical environment in which furniture and objects do not change position unexpectedly supports children's attempts to explore and map their surroundings. Using signals to identify adults (as described above) encourages children to differentiate and respond to people. To be useful to the child, the signals must be used every time the adult interacts. Skipping the stroke on the arm that means 'I'm here', and the jumping game that means 'We're here together' because the group is late for swimming may make sense to the adult, but will confuse the child. Sometimes inconsistency is unavoidable – in such situations, being aware of the case allows greater responsivity to the child's actions or reactions.

Supporting anticipation of events Sight and hearing usually supply the information necessary for anticipation. Children with multi-sensory impairment require help from adults. Consistent routines (for example, preparing to go home in the same way, in the same order each day) allow the child to build an awareness of the actions preceding a particular event. Once routines are established, the child's anticipation can be used to promote interaction – delaying fetching the coats, for example, may cause the child to prompt the adult, or move towards the coats independently. This process will not occur, however, if frequent changes prevent the child developing confidence that fetching the coats is what happens next.

Clearly marking the beginnings and ends of activities helps the child to establish where one event stops and another starts. One way of developing this is to use an object as a marker (an 'object of reference'). Helping the child carry their own towel and swimsuit from the classroom to the swimming pool, bringing them back and very clearly putting them away when swimming is finished can help to establish the boundaries. Using a range of objects to represent activities can help the child to differentiate. The objects need to be consistent (the same musical instrument each time the child goes to music), and to have meaning for the child (a seat belt clasp, for example, is more likely to identify 'bus' than a key).

Allowing time for children to receive, perceive, interpret and respond to stimuli Imperfect stimuli take longer to process (think of half-hearing a remark, then realising the meaning a second or so later). Children with multi-sensory impairment will take longer to realise who is interacting with them, longer to interpret the meaning of a message, longer to respond. They may also take longer to assimilate new experiences, and respond to teaching programmes. Sighted hearing children are aware of the actions involved in activities such as feeding long before they are expected to master them. Children with multi-sensory impairment gain meaningful experience more slowly, because of their restricted sensory input.

Giving access to activities A sighted hearing child watches adults clean their teeth, hears the water running, sees the toothpaste being squeezed onto the toothbrush, hears the adult talk about teeth being cleaned after meals. Children with multi-sensory impairment may suddenly find a hard, bristly, mint-tasting piece of plastic forced into their mouths. A coactive approach involves taking the child, adult's hands over child's hands, through the whole activity. This approach demands time and sensitivity from the adult – forcing the child to participate at an adult pace will not meet the child's needs. Working with children with multi-sensory impairment requires an acceptance that fewer things be done more slowly than we normally find appropriate.

Encouraging children to control what happens to them Viewing a child's behaviour as an adaptive response is the first step. The second is to try to identify the child's intention, and act to support this. Adults need to be aware of changes in the child's situation; differences in sensory stimuli (caused for example by the classroom door opening) may be ignored by the adult as irrelevant, but may alert or distract the child. Needing the toilet, or time passing to approach the lunch hour, may implement changes in the child's behaviour. Appropriate responses from the adult can support children's awareness that their behaviours have meaning.

Children with multi-sensory impairment lack the opportunity to learn from others' responses, and may develop signals which are outside an adult's repertoire; physical disabilities may further limit a child's attempts to signal meaning. Detailed observation may be necessary to identify and try to interpret a child's signals; video is often helpful, allowing repeated observation of one sequence of behaviour. Adults can provide situations which encourage children to realise they can affect what happens: making choices (for example, seeing, smelling and tasting two drinks to see which is preferred), requesting or refusing (wanting more of an activity, or to finish it), or breaking or delaying familiar routines to precipitate a response (Goldbart, 1988). Some children with multi-sensory impairment communicate pre-intentionally; others may use speech, signs, symbols or fingerspelling. Many children will be most appropriately served by a combination of modes.

Recognising the stress inherent in living day-to-day with multi-sensory impairment Teaching children with multi-sensory impairment is stressful; being a child with multi-sensory impairment is even more stressful. Using limited residual vision and/or hearing, or operating without these senses, is tiring and frustrating. Inconsistency is unavoidable, and self-esteem difficult to maintain in the face of limited control. Withdrawal, or refusal to co-operate, may be adaptive responses to seemingly straightforward situations.

The principles outlined here reflect a growing awareness that teaching children skills will not automatically generate their spontaneous use. Skills must be integrated into the child's understanding and control of the environment if they are to become usable as adaptive responses in new contexts. Although the examples refer to the early development of understanding, the principles hold good throughout all stages of development. A child with appropriate communicative skills may anticipate an event from being told that it will happen. The need for overt support of anticipation remains.

Most children with multi-sensory impairment have some useful residual vision and/or hearing. Information from these senses is potentially of great use to the child, but the information they provide may be distorted, fragmentary and inconsistent. Knowing how to provide the optimal auditory and visual conditions for an individual child requires assessment of both the child and the environment.

Medical information is useful, but is unlikely to suggest how children will use their senses in given situations. For children who can co-operate in assessment, clinical information is likely to be more detailed. Qualified teachers of children who are hearing impaired, visually impaired or multi-sensory impaired will be able to explain the implications of clinical information, and suggest approaches to functional assessment. One method for children at early developmental stages is to observe the child, in both familiar (often noisy and distracting) situations, and in a quiet distraction-free environment. Assessment may be structured by the use of published functional visual or auditory assessment procedures designed for this population (see for example, Langley and DuBose, 1976; Goetz *et al.*, 1982; Kershman and Napier, 1982; McInnes and Treffry, 1982; Bell, 1983). Comparison of the child's responses in the two settings will supply some information about the effects of environmental features (for example, a noisy peer, or the smell of food wafting from the kitchen). Repeated assessment is necessary to try to distinguish the various factors affecting a child's sensory functioning. The interaction and integration of information from different senses needs to be considered when planning intervention.

Environmental factors need consideration. A child with limited hearing will be more disadvantaged by background noise than one who hears fully. The child may not be able to differentiate and ignore irrelevant sounds in the way that hearing adults do. Reverberation (echo) will also affect the auditory signals received by the child. Similar considerations affect the visual environment. Big, bright, busy backgrounds, and especially people walking about, may be distracting. Lighting will greatly affect a child's use of residual vision, and changes in lighting levels (for example, between the classroom and the corridor) may cause problems. High contrast (for example, blackcurrant juice in a white cup) makes materials visually more accessible.

Many children with multi-sensory impairment need help to discover that sounds, and things seen, are meaningful. Considering experiences from the child's point of view – what materials are being offered; how they are offered; what is happening; what information is available; what is the child asked to do – clarifies some of the adaptive responses from the child. Identifying experiences which are motivating and meaningful for the child, and using these as a basis for developing responses to sensory stimuli, may prove an appropriate starting point. Every experience can be used to encourage and develop communicative awareness and skills, extending the ways in which the child understands and interacts with the world around.

Multi-sensory impairment is perhaps the most difficult disability to imagine. It creates enormous disadvantage, and vastly complex needs. Meeting the needs requires family support, an empathetic approach which views the child's behaviours as meaningful adaptive responses, multi-disciplinary expertise supporting appropriate assessment and intervention, realistic staffing levels allowing attachment and a coactive approach and appropriate physical environments and equipment. These requirements are by no means available to all children with multi-sensory impairment, but recognition of the needs, and moves towards appropriate provision, have expanded hugely in recent years. With appropriate provision, there is no reason why children should not learn to understand and control at least a limited environment.

REFERENCES

Ainsworth, M.D.S., Blehar, M., Waters, E. and Wall, E. (1978) *Patterns of Attachment*, Hillsdale, NJ: Erlbaum.

Bell, J. (1983) 'Assessment of visual ability in the profoundly handicapped', *Newsletter of the National Association of Deaf-Blind Rubella Handicapped*, 29, 3, 16–17.

Best, C. (1983) 'The "new" deaf-blind?', *British Journal of Visual Impairment*, 1, 2, 11–13.

Department of Education and Science (1989) *Educational Provision for Deaf-Blind Children*, London: DES.

Fox, A.M. (1983) 'The effects of combined vision and hearing loss on the attainment of developmental milestones', paper given at the First Canadian Conference on the Education and Development of Deaf-Blind Infants and Children, W. Ross Macdonald School, Brantford, Ontario.

Goetz, L., Utley, B., Gee, K., Baldwin, M. and Sailor, W. (1982) *Auditory Assessment and Programming Manual for Severely Handicapped and Deaf-Blind Students*, Seattle: The Association for the Severely Retarded.

Goldbart, J. (1988) 'Communication for a purpose', in J. Coupe and J. Goldbart (eds) *Communication Before Speech*, Beckenham, Kent: Croom Helm.

Great Britain (1989) *Education (Teachers) Regulations 1989* (SI 1989/1319).

Hills, J. (1991) 'A way forward', *Talking Sense*, 37, 1, 8–11.

Kershman, S.M. and Napier, D. (1982) 'Systematic procedures for eliciting and recording responses to sound stimuli in deaf-blind multi-handicapped children', *Volta Review*, 84, 4, 226–37.

Lamb, M.E. (1981) 'The development of social expectations in the first year of life', in M.E. Lamb and L.R. Sherrold (eds) *Infant Social Cognition: Empirical and Theoretical Considerations*, Hillsdale, NJ: Erlbaum.

Langley, M.B. and DuBose, R.F. (1976) 'Functional vision screening for severely handicapped children', *New Outlook for the Blind*, 70, 8, 346–50.

McInnes, J.M. and Treffry, J.A. (1982) *Deaf-Blind Infants and Children*, Milton Keynes: Open University Press.

Nafstad, A. (1989) *Space of Interaction: An Attempt to Understand How Congenital Deaf-Blindness Affects Psychological Development*, Dronninglund, Denmark: Nordic Staff Training Centre for Deaf-Blind Services.

Siegel-Causey, E. and Downing, J. (1987) 'Nonsymbolic communication development: theoretical concepts and educational strategies', in L. Goetz, D. Guess and K. Stremel-Campbell (eds) *Innovative Program Design for Individuals with Dual Sensory Impairments*, Baltimore: Paul H. Brookes.

Smith, A.J. and Shane Cote, K. (1982) *Look At Me: A Resource Manual for the Development of Residual Vision in Multiply Impaired Children*, Philadelphia: Pennsylvania College of Optometry.

van Dijk, J. (1986) 'An educational curriculum for deaf-blind multi-handicapped persons', in D. Ellis (ed.) *Sensory Impairments in Mentally Handicapped People*, Beckenham, Kent: Croom Helm.

——(1989) 'The Sint Michielsgestel approach to diagnosis and education of multisensory impaired persons', paper given at Warwick '89: Sensory Impairment with Multi-Handicap, Warwick University.

——(1991) *Persons Handicapped by Rubella: Victors and Victims – a Follow-Up Study*, Amsterdam: Swets and Zeitlinger.

Visser, T. (1988) 'Educational programming for deaf-blind children: some important topics', *Deaf-Blind Education*, 2, 4–7.

Writer, J. (1987) 'A movement-based approach to the education of students who are sensory impaired/multihandicapped', in L. Goetz, D. Guess and K. Stremel-Campbell (eds) *Innovative Program Design for Individuals with Dual Sensory Impairments*, Baltimore: Paul H. Brookes.

Wyman, R. (1986) *Multiply Handicapped Children*, London: Souvenir Press.

NAME INDEX

SUBJECT INDEX

anorexia 145
arthritis 154
assessment: psychometric 21;
    curriculum based 21–5, 29–32;
    in National Curriculum 23–5, 30;
    of special needs: hearing
    impairment 136–8, 143–4;
    multi-sensory impairment
    194–5; severe learning
    difficulties 63; speech and
    language difficulties 88–90;
    visual impairment 114–16
asthma 157–8
astigmatism 116
ataxia 151
athetosis 151
autism 61, 63–4

behaviour difficulties: see
    emotional and behaviour
    difficulties
blindness: see visual impairment
brain damage 152
brittle bone disease 154

cerebral palsy 151–3
challenging behaviour 67
child abuse 165, 172–8 physical
    173–34; emotional 174–75;
    neglect 175–76; sexual 176–78
chromosomal abnormalities 64
classroom management 37–8, 45,
    107, 117–24, 144–5
cleft palate 82

clumsy children 52
collaboration 38, 45, 69–70
conductive education 162
counselling 38, 103
curriculum 3, 13–25, 34–5, 52–67,
    124–45; see National Curriculum
cystic fibrosis 158

deaf: see hearing impairment
deaf-blind: see multisensory
    impairment
diabetes 158–9
disruptive pupils 93–7
Downs syndrome 64
dyslexia 45–52

ecosystemic approach 104–5
Edith Norrie letter case 50
Education Act (1981) 7–9, 17, 19,
    29–31, 66, 106, 111, 136
Education Reform Act (1988) 14,
    20, 21, 29, 32, 71
educational TV 55
Elton Committee of Enquiry 96–8
emotional and behaviour
    difficulties: conceptions of
    93–99; provisions 105–7;
    approaches: behaviourism
    100–2; psycho-therapy 102–3;
    ecosystemic 103–105
epilepsy 159–160

family roles 165–166
Fernald kinaesthetic method 49–50